JOSHUA
Mighty Warrior and Man of Faith

Books by W. Phillip Keller

Splendor from the Sea
As a Tree Grows
Bold under God— *A Fond Look at a Frontier Preacher*
A Shepherd Looks at Psalm 23
A Layman Looks at the Lord's Prayer
Rabboni— Which Is to Say, Master
A Shepherd Looks at the Good Shepherd and His Sheep
A Gardener Looks at the Fruits of the Spirit
Mighty Man of Valor— Gideon
Mountain Splendor
Taming Tension
Expendable
Still Waters
A Child Looks at Psalm 23
Ocean Glory
Walking with God
On Wilderness Trails
Elijah— Prophet of Power
Salt for Society
A Layman Looks at the Lamb of God
Lessons from a Sheep Dog
Wonder o' the Wind
Joshua— Mighty Warrior and Man of Faith
A Layman Looks at the Love of God
Sea Edge
David I
David II
Sky Edge
Chosen Vessels
In the Master's Hands
Predators in Our Pulpits
Songs of My Soul
Thank You, Father
God Is My Delight

JOSHUA
Mighty Warrior and Man of Faith

W. Phillip Keller

Grand Rapids, MI 49501

Joshua: Mighty Warrior and Man of Faith

© 1983, 1992 by W. Phillip Keller

Published by Kregel Publications, a division of Kregel, Inc.,
P.O. Box 2607, Grand Rapids, MI 49501. Kregel Publications
provides trusted, biblical publications for Christian growth and
service. Your comments and suggestions are valued.

Cover design: Alan G. Hartman

For more information about Kregel Publications, visit our
web site at: www.kregel.com

Library of Congress Cataloging-in-Publication Data
Keller, W. Phillip (Weldon Phillip), 1920–1997
   [Joshua, man of fearless faith]
   Joshua: mighty warrior and man of faith / by W. Phillip
Keller.
   p.   cm.
   Reprint: Originally published: Joshua, man of fearless
faith, Waco, TX: Word Books, © 1983.
   1. Joshua (Bible figure). 2. Bible, O.T.—Biography.
3. Bible, O.T. Hexateuch—Devotional literature.
I. Title. II. Title: Joshua, mighty warrior and man of faith.

BS580.J7K44   1992   222'.2092—dc20   91-21649
                                                       CIP
ISBN 0-8254-2999-4

Printed in the United States of America
4 5 6 7 / 04 03

To
all those faithful people both in
Canada and the United States
who shared the study of
Joshua's life
with me

Acknowledgments

A NOTE OF THANKS must be given to both Mr. Lacey in British Columbia, and Mr. and Mrs. Hugh Petersen of California for providing me with tapes of the Bible studies we shared together.

I am also grateful to both the First Baptist Church of Penticton, B.C., and the Montecito Covenant Church of Montecito, California, for opening their facilities for these community-wide studies.

My dear wife, Ursula, has typed the manuscript with care and accuracy. She also listened patiently to my reading the rough manuscript to her, for which I am grateful.

I have often paraphrased Scripture in the interest of dramatizing the events that take place in Joshua's life. These paraphrases do not have Scripture references.

My own spiritual life has been energized and stimulated by the bold example of Joshua's fearless faith in God. I do thank my Father in heaven for this uplift and encouragement from His Word.

Contents

Foreword

CERTAIN PEOPLE stand head and shoulders above their peers in the biblical narrative. Joshua is one of those people. It is not his physical stature that causes him to stand out—it is his spiritual character. Joshua stood alone in his day and time as the protege of Moses. The mantle of Moses passed on to him with scarcely a ripple—because Joshua was, in many ways, God's man for that hour.

First of all, Joshua was obedient. He was willing to do God's bidding without question—and he was willing to put his life on the line in carrying out God's plan and purpose.

Second, even though his name does not appear in God's "hall of faith" in Hebrews 11, Joshua was a man of faith. He learned well at the feet of his mentor, Moses, what it meant to *believe* God—and to venture out on the basis of that faith.

Third, Joshua combined the unlikely elements of statesman, soldier and saint. He was filled with the Spirit of God (Deuteronomy 34:9). The Word of God filled his inner man (Joshua

1:8). And he also practiced the presence of God in his daily life
(Joshua 1:5; 6:27).

Interestingly enough, if I were to think of a modern man who
personified many of the traits I have come to associate with
Joshua, that man would be Phillip Keller, the author of this
book. He has the same kind of rugged courage and fearless faith
that Joshua did, the same willingness to obey God regardless of
personal cost.

I first met Phillip Keller nearly a quarter of a century ago,
even before he wrote his timeless classic, *A Shepherd Looks at
Psalm 23.* Since that time our paths have crossed countless
times, and I have had the joy of working closely with Phillip on
some of his later books, the most recent of which was *Lessons
from a Sheep Dog.* Down through the years Phillip has im-
pressed me as a man with a message—and one who forthrightly
lives out that message in his own life style. He is also uniquely a
man's man, a man comfortable in the presence of other men
but uncomfortable in the "drawing room" atmosphere of
society.

Above all, Phillip Keller is God's man, a man of the Book—
and he believes and lives out the principles and precepts of that
Word without compromise or hesitation. In the pages of
Joshua I often saw the man Phillip Keller—and I highly recom-
mend him to you the reader. I believe the insights shared in
this biography have implications and blessings for modern
man—if he will hearken to them—and I heartily applaud this
book as a look into the life of a man with much to say to our
modern day. It is a book for men—that women just might
appreciate as well!

AL BRYANT

The Background

GOD, OUR FATHER, has given us formidable lessons in faith clearly displayed in the life of Joshua. He moves through the early history of Israel in quiet strength with significant success. His character and his conduct gleam like threads of gold woven into the dark tapestry of his times.

Often overshadowed by the exploits of Moses, frequently forgotten in the wilderness wanderings of his wayward contemporaries, Joshua stands steady in fearless faith. He portrays for us the person in whom God is well pleased. He demonstrates the fearless faith in the Almighty which is always honored with remarkable results.

The incredible story of Israel's release and exodus from slavery in the slime pits of Egypt is the story of every soul set free from bondage to sin and Satan. The dreadful sojourn in the desert wastes on the way to the Land of Promise is the saga of a soul that wanders in the wilderness of a divided mind, divided affections, divided will.

The final triumphant entry into the land flowing with milk and honey is the victorious song of the soul that triumphs in

Christ. It displays the overcoming life of the soul set free from self, finding fulfillment and rest in God's place of provision. Against the background of a stubborn, stiff-necked nation moving reluctantly and in rebellion against God's will, we watch, amazed, as this mighty man prepared to carry out God's commands at any cost. Despite the dark unbelief all around him, despite the rebellion of his people, despite the dreadful delays of forty desert years, Joshua emerges triumphant. He is the commanding character who finds his faith in God vindicated in resounding victories.

Let us learn from his example!

1

The First Victory

THE LORD GOD, Jehovah, had released the nation of Israel from their serfdom to Pharaoh in a titanic display of divine power. Plague after plague had engulfed Egypt in horror and death. Frogs and flies, darkness and disease had ravaged, polluted and crippled the country. Ultimately, upon the awesome visitation of the destroying angel, all the firstborn of the land were annihilated. Only those whose homes were sheltered by the blood of a sacrificial lamb, sprinkled upon the door posts and lintel, were spared in that horrendous hour.

Moving en masse, some two million Israelis, almost half as many as occupy Israel today, streamed out of their houses, headed toward the dawn breaking over the eastern desert. They were on their way back to their homeland in Palestine, in Canaan. This land of promise, fertile, well watered, beautifully wooded, had been given to Abraham, Isaac and Jacob, their patriarchs, as a covenant inheritance from the Almighty.

Had they taken the shortest and most direct route, the journey could have been accomplished in about fourteen days, even moving ever so slowly because of their tiny tots and lowing, bleating herds of livestock. Instead, the desert crossing, the long tedious trek through the Sinai peninsula and across the mideastern Arab wastes, was to occupy forty years of dreadful wilderness wanderings.

Of the two million souls who moved out of Egypt under the mighty hand of God, only two men, Joshua and Caleb, and their families, would survive to set foot in Canaan. A ratio of roughly only one in a million of this intransigent nation would have sufficient faith in God to ever be granted the triumph of taking territory in the Promised Land across Jordan.

In a remarkable succession of incredible events, the gigantic Exodus from Egypt went ahead under divine protection. A safe passage was provided across the headwaters of the Red Sea. The pursuing horsemen and war chariots of Egypt's famous cavalry were engulfed and drowned in the rushing waters that closed behind the Israelis.

In the desert marches a peculiar, awesome pillar of fire hovered above the moving multitude by night. It gave protection and light in the dark. By it they could travel at night when conditions were cool. During the day a majestic white cloud covered the camp, sheltering and shading the transients from the desert's burning sun. As though under a magnificent umbrella, covering thousands of acres of land, men and livestock could rest in its shade.

Even more astonishing was the sudden appearance of manna in the morning. Food of divine origin, it lay white, shimmering and sweet upon the ground. Like silver dew that spangles the grass at dawn, the bread from above was a beautiful sight that guaranteed health, strength and vitality for the families who went out to gather it six days each week.

Despite the difficult desert trails with their rough rocks, burning sands, abrasive stones and eternal dust the traveler's sandals showed no wear or tear. In spite of sticks and thorns and scrub cactus the people tramped the wilderness wastes without discomfort to their weary feet.

As with their sandals, so with their cl··· ··· ¡e apparel they
brought with them from E··· ··· their wearers
were buried in ··· ··· if it was forty
da··· ··· ¡te the dust,
de··· ··· erspiration,
the···

In··· ··· had never
been··· ··· ¡o million
peopl··· ··· ¡weled in
compa··· ··· eep and
cattle, ··· ··· Guided
by God··· ··· ¡, they
moved ¡··· ··· south
toward t···

Moses··· ··· ¡brew
family, his··· ··· ¡ude
basket crad··· ··· ¡¡u him in the
dense papy··· ··· ¡¡ud flats. There he was
discovered b··· ···¡aughter, a royal princess. Her femi-
nine instincts ···¡¡stored the infant to his own family until he was
weaned of his mother's milk.

Then, adopted as a regal son into the royal household of
Egypt, Moses grew up and matured into a full-fledged prince
of the Pharaohs. Carefully he was groomed and fitted as a
fighting man of war, skilled in all the ancient arts and science of
Egypt's proud civilization. He was taught the martial arts, the
military strategies, the proud traditions of this desert nation.
For forty years he lived as a royal prince.

Still he never forgot his humble Hebrew roots. One day in a
blinding fit of rage he slaughtered an Egyptian who abused one
of his own Israelis. Secretly he buried the body in the sand. But
he had been seen! In fear for his very life he fled down to these
same southern desert wastes where now his people camped.

There for another forty, long, tedious, trying years the

prince of Egypt cared for sheep and goats as a nomadic desert herder. Then one day, arrested by the spectacle of a bush that burned but did not disappear in smoke and ash, he heard the call of God. It was his commissioning to return to Egypt; to lead his people out of bondage to the Pharaohs; to bring them across these wilderness trails he knew so well; to take them safely to the land of Canaan flowing with milk and honey.

So now they reached Rephidim, a forbidding, fierce place encircled with burning rock cliffs, yet without water, either for man or beast. Its very name was pregnant with pity—*"Where weakened hands hang down."* A spot of despair and discouragement for Israel.

For the second time in a matter of just a few days, the irritable Israelis found fault with Moses. The first time it had been because they feared their food supplies were exhausted. With anger, vehemence and false accusations they charged their leader with bringing them into the desert to die with hunger.

God's divine intervention was to provide the honey-sweet manna in the morning. And at sunset flocks of desert quail flew into the camp to satisfy the travelers' hunger for meat. Still somehow they failed to feel secure or satisfied in Jehovah's care.

Now again at Rephidim, with no water in sight, they were sure they and their stock would die of thirst. Rendered griefstricken by their anger, beside himself with their unbelief and lack of trust in God's guidance, the enraged Moses shouted back, "Why do you taunt God with your tirade?"

Despite all the mighty miracles displayed in their deliverance from the grim brickyards of Egypt; despite all the divine conquest of Egypt's military might; despite the pillar of fire by night, the cloud by day; despite the provision of manna and quail and imperishable clothing for the way—this intransigent nation blatantly charged both Moses and God with duplicity and the intent to commit mass murder.

In self-pity and self-centered preoccupation with their plight, they failed to see or recognize the faithfulness of their God. In crass and blind belligerence they heaped abuse on Moses, who in fact stood before them as God's man and God's spokesman.

Again Jehovah was gracious enough to give them water from a barren rock. Unfortunately for Moses, in anger at Israel's attitude, instead of merely commanding water to come forth he struck the stone with repeated blows. Water gushed out, but God had been grieved.

The spot was called Massah and Meribah where Israel challenged the goodness of God and there found fault with His direction of their destiny. In gross self-pity they had charged God with intending to destroy them. Here was the cause of their dismay, the source of their utter discouragement. It was but another of the low points of despair that would characterize the unstable, unpredictable up-and-down character of this self-willed nation.

What was true of Israel here as an entire people, is so often applicable to us as individual souls. In our selfish preoccupation with our recurring problems in life we turn to intense self-pity. We indulge our emotions in the outrage of challenging God's capacity to really care for us. We wallow in the gross ingratitude of forgetting our Father's past faithfulness in providing for us. We taunt and try Him by deliberately doubting that He can deliver us from our present dilemma.

Seen in this light we can begin to understand the serious dimensions of the evil of our unbelief. Surely self-pity is the most heinous of all human sins in the sight of God. In its manifestation, this attitude of soul shows clearly a person's total self-preoccupation with self-centered reliance. God's power,

God's person, God's presence is ruled out to the extent where, as with Israel, the cruel question is asked in disbelief: "Is God even here?"—"Does He even care?"

It is precisely at this low point that we stand in peril, discouraged, dismayed, downcast. Nor are we ever more vulnerable to attack.

In the case of Israel it was the fierce desert tribe of Amalek who decided to launch an attack.

Amalek, like Israel, was a desert nation, the fierce descendants from Abraham and Isaac through the lineage of Esau, Jacob's older twin brother. Always they would oppose Israel. Always they would attempt to annihilate the offspring of Jacob. Always there would be war between them, from generation to generation.

The Amalekites fought with the Midianites against Gideon. They were the archenemy God commanded King Saul to wipe out. It was Haman, an Amalekite, who planned to destroy the Hebrews in the days of Queen Esther.

Amalek in the Old Testament record represents our *old self.* He stands for the unrelenting war that rages within the soul of man between the Spirit of God and *the flesh.* This is the eternal opposition of our stubborn *old nature* to the best purposes of God in our lives.

Moses called in Joshua, a relatively young man of only about forty years, and commanded him to assemble a force with which to go into battle at once. There would be war the very next day. This was no easy assignment. Joshua was not a military commander. Like his companions he had spent his young life in the slime pits of Egypt making bricks for Pharaoh. His battle experience was nil, his use of arms minimal.

Yet the amazing thing was Joshua's prompt response. He did not delay! He did not offer up excuses for not going into action. He did not plead inexperience or lack of military training.

Instead he simply set out to do this impossible assignment with alacrity.

Immediately this gives us the key to the man's remarkable character. He combined complete obedience to God's will with a resolute faith that Jehovah would empower him to carry out His commands.

In a word, Joshua had an unshakable assurance in the Lord God. Whatever God asked of him, he would do without fear.

The very name "Joshua" bears within it this noble stance: *"Jehovah (God) is salvation."* It is God Himself who saves. It is God who delivers. It is God, very God, who grants glorious victory óver the enemy.

While Joshua and his hand-picked men clashed in ferocious combat with Amalek, Moses climbed to a height of land to pray for his young rookies fighting in the desert below. It was a bloodbath that raged back and forth all day in the hot sun. Men fell on both sides, their lifeblood spilling out from ghastly sword wounds to stain the desert sands and stones. As long as Moses held his hands aloft, outstretched toward heaven, beseeching God's power in this place where the hands of others had hung down, there was victory. But when his arms, too, grew weary and hung heavy by his side Joshua and his men were in jeopardy. So two of Moses' closest associates joined him in lifting up his hands to God: Aaron his brother on one side, and Hur, his brother-in-law on the other side.

Finally, by sundown, when the desert sun sank as a red and flaming ball of fire into the dark waters of the Red Sea to the west, victory came to Joshua and the young men with him. It had been their baptism into battle to the death. It had been their first ferocious encounter with a fierce enemy force. And Joshua emerged triumphant in victory over the vanquished. He had turned tragedy into triumph for all of Israel.

As a memorial to commemorate this great initial victory,

God commanded Moses to record it in his writings. He was to rehearse it often to the young Joshua as a reminder of God's presence with His people in great power.

There an altar of honor was erected by Moses to the glory of God. He called it *"Jehovah–Nissi"*—meaning "The Lord is My Banner." It was the presence of the Almighty, prevailing in power, who raised aloft the standard of His Spirit to overcome the enemy, to give victory to His own people in their hour of struggle.

There is much for us as God's people to learn from this first great victory of Joshua's. The basic spiritual principles which applied at Rephidim remain steadfast and unchanged to this very hour.

First, we are not to indulge ourselves in the despicable practice of self-pity. Nor are we to sympathize with those who do. Our role in life is to trust God, no matter how difficult the situation may appear. We are not here to dispute our dilemma with Him, nor challenge His capacity to care for us, nor question His management of our affairs.

Second, we do not look for someone else to blame for our difficulties. If we are truly walking with Christ, led by His Spirit, there are bound to be some dark days. But they are of His arrangement and He can readily bring great blessing to us even out of a seemingly desert wasteland.

Third, the Word of the Lord to us will ever be to do battle with Amalek (our old self-nature). There is to be no ceasefire, no armistice arrangement, no respite from a ruthless warfare with ourselves. We are our own worst enemy when it comes to accomplishing God's best intentions for us. Our old selfish desires must be put to death.

Fourth, whatever the Lord God commands us to do we should undertake at once. True faith in Him is my personal, positive response to His Word, to the point where I act upon it and simply do what He commands. I do not look for excuses, offer weak-kneed apologies for my incompetence, or debate the issue with God. I simply obey and accede to His authority.

Last of all, as friends and associates lift up holy hands to God, agreed together on behalf of victory in the battles of life, God will grant power and might to overcome. The honor is His. The acclaim is His. The victory is His. The great strides forward in the face of formidable opposition are His arrangement. Glory be to His name who causes us to triumph through Christ Jesus (2 Corinthians 2:14).

2
Three Vignettes of Joshua's Character

THE MASSED COMPANY of Israel, along with tents, cattle, sheep and goats, had moved on across the desert from the rugged rocks of Rephidim. Now they were encamped at the foot of Mount Sinai. This gaunt and rugged mountain where God chose to reveal Himself to Moses came to be known as "The Holy Mount." It was a craggy peak that smoked and thundered ominously when the power of the Almighty was made manifest upon it.

It was on Mount Sinai that God, very God, would inscribe in stone the remarkable decalogue of the ten divine commandments. These were the expressed will and wish of Jehovah for the welfare and well being of His special and chosen people. They conveyed His best intentions for the best interests of Israel. They are rules of personal conduct designed for the supreme benefit of all men of all time. The passage of nearly 3500 years of human history since that remarkable event has not diminished the value or validity of those supreme, spiritual standards for human conduct.

So awesome was the supernatural power and energy of God's imminence upon the mountain that all the people were warned not to set foot upon it. Even the livestock herders were not to graze their herds upon the slopes for they would surely perish in its close proximity. Though Israel was a chosen people, a peculiar treasure, a separate race selected for God's ultimate purposes on the planet, this gave them no license to undue familiarity or casual conduct with their Deliverer. He was their God, very God, to be held in holy reverence and respectful awe.

Only when special burnt offerings and sacrificial peace offerings had been made, with the shed blood sprinkled on both the crude altar of uncut stones and on the people, could their elders approach the mountain (Exodus 24). Their safety and their security were established by the blood shed on their behalf.

It was on the slopes of this stern mountain that God would commune with Moses, face to face, as friend to friend. Covered by dense clouds, enclosed in the enfolding majesty of the Most High, here Jehovah would deliver to His appointed leader all the social mores and laws for their communal conduct. Enfolded in the splendor of His own wondrous presence He would here instruct Moses in all the details regarding the construction of a portable tabernacle with all of its attendant sacrifices and priestly duties.

This was a high and holy calling. To accomplish all His best purposes for His people, the Lord God commanded Moses to come up into His presence upon the rugged peak. It was an order that would have utterly intimidated most men. But not Moses! Without hesitation he chose one young, courageous companion from all of Israel, Joshua, and climbed the slopes into the clouds.

The two men disappeared into the swirling gray mists of commingled cloud, smoke and darkness like two fearless mountaineers set for the final assault on the summit. Moses' remarkable last words to his elders were, *"We (Joshua and I)*

will come again; tarry here until our return!" It was like a
distant echo of Abraham's final remark to his servants when he
and Isaac pushed on alone to the top of Mount Moriah (Genesis
22:5).

For forty long days and forty dreadful nights there was no
sign of the two men. Only the ominous thunderings of the
smoking mountain broke the silence. Only the eerie glow of
the awesome glory of the celestial fire lit the night sky. Only
the swirling shrouds of heavy cloud swirled about the summit
during the day.

Moses was in constant, close communion with God.

Joshua was utterly alone, waiting in silence for his master!

It is a measure of the man's magnificent moral fortitude that
he did not despair or give way to panic in his solitude. It is a
tribute to the unshakable faith he had in God that he did not
break under the strain and retreat down the slopes alone to
rejoin his friends at the foot of the mount. It is a mark of
Joshua's sterling character that despite his own desperate hunger and thirst during the forty-day fast he never deserted
Moses to indulge his own burning desires.

Moses' mind, emotions, spirit and will were actively preoccupied with all the intricate instructions imparted to him by
Jehovah. By contrast, Joshua had nothing but his own quiet
confidence in God to sustain his strength, physical, emotional
and spiritual, during this staggering sojourn. Through it all he
remained utterly loyal, tough as fire-tested steel, unshakable
in his fearless faith.

There is a remarkable lesson here for all of us. It is stated
best in the form of a forthright question. "What is the caliber of
my character?" Too many of us will not, cannot seem to trust
God in the silent interludes of life. Most of us can show fortitude, faith, even bravery in the heroic crises of life. Yet we are
called of Christ, at other times, to come apart from our comrades and associates, to be alone with Him in seclusion, to

seem even forgotten for awhile. Can we also be loyal, faithful, steadfast then?

Joshua could! His compatriots camped at the base of the mountain could not!

After waiting a few weeks for Moses and Joshua to reappear, the Israelis grew weary of their vigil. They assumed some catastrophe had overtaken Moses on the mountain. He and Joshua would not be back. What further use in waiting for their return? Why not devise some sort of substitute god who would be tangible and visible, to lead them out of their quandary? In fact it could even be fun to fashion a deity that made no great demands on their devotion to him.

So the petulant people pressed Aaron with their demands. They insisted that since he was the high priest he should come up with a substitute deity they could worship. In fear for his own life Aaron capitulated to their demands. He ordered them to divest themselves of all the gold jewelry they had borrowed from the Egyptians. With it he would fashion in the fire a golden bull calf.

In Egyptian mythology bulls were sacred beasts. In their spiritual delusion the people of the Nile believed the earth was upheld in space upon the massive backs of four strong bulls. Each faced in one of the four directions of the quadrant: north, south, east and west. In honor and memory of this absurd mythology Aaron turned the attention of Israel back to the dreadful deception and degradation of their former slave masters.

By actually devising, shaping and sculpting the golden bull calf he was also blatantly breaking the very first and foremost command given to Israel by Jehovah God: "Thou shalt have no other gods before me. Thou shalt not make unto thee any graven image (shaped with a tool)" (Exodus 20:1–6).

In wild abandon the people responded by singing and shouting defiantly in obeisance to the bull. They danced around it in an orgy of sensual depravity. All as if to say—"Here is our god. Here is our deliverer. Here is our licentious leader."

On the mountain, amid the mists, amid the cloud, amid the incandescent glow of the grandeur of God, there came up the sounds of the rebellious revelry at its base. Jehovah God ordered Moses to return to his proud, willful, stiff-necked associates. In less that six short weeks they had forgotten His faithfulness to them. In a matter of forty days they had completely corrupted themselves (Exodus 32).

It is the same old, tired, tragic story of man's intransigence and perversion despite the gracious generosity of a caring God. It is the continuous replay of historic drama of human degradation in spite of God's call to noble life. It is the acute revelation to our spirits of the total depravity of human nature as opposed to the sublime integrity of a loving Lord.

Hurrying down the mountain as fast as he could, bearing in his hands the two stone tablets engraved by the finger of God, Moses remarked to Joshua that he thought he could hear the distant sounds of singing coming from the camp below.

Joshua's reply to Moses gives us a tremendous insight into the depths of this young man's spiritual perception. *"There is a noise of war in the camp!"*

Better than his elder, Joshua immediately grasped the enormity of the evil precipitated by the perverse people caught up in their idol worship. With remarkable sensitivity to the titanic spiritual struggle now under way Joshua knew there was war between man and God. The superficial singing, the strident shouting, the horrible dances were but a front, a facade to mask the flagrant effrontery to God Almighty.

Moses, a more pragmatic person than his servant Joshua, was sure the sounds he heard were only revelry and pleasure. Joshua, attuned and in harmony with the mind of God knew in a much deeper dimension that here was a profound spiritual battle that would end in terrible consequences for Israel.

Israel, a people called out of the darkness and slavery of Egypt, had stumbled back into the slime pits of sin and perversion as surely as a sow returns to wallow in the mud. Called of God to be a separate people, a unique race, a precious treasure to Himself, they had betrayed His trust, trampled on His goodness, forfeited His divine favor.

In anguish God had, at first, been inclined to annihilate them. But Moses interceded on their behalf, prevailing upon the Lord to withhold His stern retribution and spare them as a nation.

But when Moses came close enough to actually see what Israel had done in diametrical disobedience to God's wishes, he flung the tablets of stone in fury at the foot of the mountain. They shattered down the rock slopes like the hot anger that spewed from his soul.

In a rage he challenged Aaron to explain how or why he could be so obtuse, so wicked, so perverted by this perverse people. The excuses only enraged Moses further. He was beside himself in loyalty to God with whom he had been in communion on the mount.

In a burst of fearless courage he challenged all of Israel to decide that very hour whether or not any were for or against God. "Who is on the LORD's side?" (Exodus 32:26) he shouted vehemently.

In response to his stirring call all the sons of Levi, the budding priests of Israel, rallied to their leader's side. He ordered each man armed. Then in a frenzy of dire judgment each was ordered to take sword in hand and slaughter the offenders.

It was a dreadful day. By sundown about 3000 of their fellow men lay dead upon the desert sands. The people were paralyzed with terror and fear. Nor was the end of the grim reprisal in sight had not Moses intervened and begged God to forgive Israel their awful iniquity (Exodus 32).

Still judgment came. A terrible plague fell upon the people.

Many more perished and it was known indeed that there was war between God and man at the foot of the mount. A fearsome price was paid for the pride and arrogance of a people who had set themselves against God.

Broken, humbled and contrite, the children of Israel now stripped themselves of all their ornaments and finery. Any sign that they would flaunt God or disregard His commands were swept away in an attitude of penitence and prayer.

Moses himself, utterly distraught in heart, grieved in spirit, wished to disassociate himself from this intransigent people. He had the special sanctuary tent, which served as a temporary tabernacle, moved outside the camp. There, separate from the Israelis, he sought the face of God again. Whenever he entered this holy trysting place with the Almighty, the cloudy pillar of God's presence descended and stood at the entrance to it.

It was in this special spot that Joshua, the young man so loyal to Moses and so devoted to God, chose deliberately to stay. In fact it is startling to discover that he made this tabernacle his residence (Exodus 33:11). He had decided that he, too, preferred to be totally identified with God Himself in His house, rather than with his rebellious countrymen.

Such a decision had far-reaching implications for young Joshua. No longer was he just another one of the crowd. Nor was he just a common man. He was an individual to whom the will and purposes of God were supremely paramount. He was a man who had placed a special priority upon spiritual issues and God's eternal interests. This would entail loneliness, separation, and even isolation from his associates. Yet in his genuine and faithful dedication to the Lord, this was a price he was not afraid to pay.

From these brief, salient insights into the character of Joshua we see a man willing to be loyal, faithful and sincere in his subservient role as a servant to Moses and to God. Having thus demonstrated his reliability, even in the most difficult and tough trials, it is little wonder he would later be chosen by God for great leadership and mighty victories that would overshadow his predecessors.

Faithful in small things, he would be put in command of stirring conquests yet to come.

3

Joshua the Spy for God

ISRAEL, BY A succession of fits and starts, had slowly moved northward from Sinai toward Canaan. As before there had been repeated complaints from the camp. This strange nation of God's choice was never contented with conditions as they found them. Grumbling, fault finding, hankering for their old life style in Egypt on the mud flats of the Nile, they were a pain to God and a perplexity to Moses.

Somehow, in a cantankerous, obtuse way, they had the twisted habit of forgetting the whips and lashes, the sweat and labor of bowed backs, in the brutal brickyards of Egypt. All they could remember were the taste of leeks, garlic, onions and lentils between their teeth and under their tongues. They savored again the flesh of the fish caught in the murky waters of the great mother river that flooded their flat, delta lowlands.

To assuage their lust, and silence their whining, God arranged for massive flights of desert quail to come inland from the edge of the Red Sea. The people gathered them in huge quantities, only to have the flesh become putrid and contaminated so that they were smitten with a dreadful disease. What they had lusted for they had received until it turned to their own ruin. Their souls were left lean because of it.

It is dangerous to demand anything from the Lord. In our human fallibility we often try to force the hand of God. So frequently we are sure we know best. The truth is we do not. Yet He will acquiesce to our persistent petitions. For only in this way can He demonstrate to us that our limited knowledge and fallible understanding can lead to serious consequences. Thus He hopes to teach us to trust Him implicitly.

Amid this episode with his willful, wayward people Moses had reached the extremity of his patience with their petulance. In a fit of utter frustration he pled for God to snuff out his spirit and grant him release from the relentless burden of Israel's intransigence. Their constant anger, belligerence and grievances against God's guidance were more than he could bear alone.

In compassion Jehovah instructed Moses to gather seventy select men who were the more stable leaders amongst the people. These were to assemble outside the camp at the tabernacle where Moses and Joshua met with the Almighty. There God saw fit to dispense His divine Spirit upon the entire group of men. Thus they would be empowered to help bear the burden of administering this difficult and irritable group of people.

Part of their responsibility was to prophesy to their contemporaries. That is to declare fearlessly the word of the Lord and thus convey His intentions to the listeners. It so happened two of the elite group, Eldad and Medad, began to speak on God's behalf while still in the camp. This was a most unusual occurrence that promptly drew public attention. At once a young man rushed off to report the incident to Moses and Joshua in the tabernacle.

Joshua, so loyal to his leader Moses, so zealous to retain the honor of both God's appointed chief and His holy tabernacle, found the action in the camp unacceptable. His enormous reverence and respect for the presence and power of Jehovah constrained him to ask Moses to silence the two men in camp.

Instead Moses cut his young commander short with the bit-ing comment, "Are you envious for my sake? Would to God all His people were prophets, and that He would put His Spirit upon all of them!"

It was a hasty, ill-conceived retort to young Joshua.

First, it showed a genuine lack of appreciation on Moses' part for the acute and intense loyalty of his young lieutenant. Second, it demonstrated that Joshua already knew better than his leader that God's gracious Spirit is given only to those who obey Him and comply with His wishes. His Spirit simply is not shared with the masses who have no intention of complying with the Lord's intentions.

Already Joshua had seen the dire judgment of divine wrath fall upon Nadab and Abihu, sons of Aaron who in audacity offered strange fire before the Lord. In an incandescent con-flagration they were consumed before the people. God's ex-plicit command on that occasion, through Moses, was that no one upon whom the anointing oil reposed dared go out of the tabernacle door (Leviticus 10).

So Joshua now trembled for his associates in the camp. He held in awesome respect the commands of God. And this ex-plains why in due course it was he himself who would be chosen as the supreme commander to succeed Moses. No other man in all of Israel was so dedicated to doing God's will or carrying out His commands.

It is appropriate to pause here and point out that to be so single-minded in one's loyalty to the Lord is not to be bound by some burdensome legal bondage. Many Christians have this erroneous notion. Rather it is the person who carries out Christ's command, who complies with His wishes, who capitu-lates whole-heartedly (i.e. with his will) to Christ's instruc-tions, who truly loves Him (Read John 14 and 15).

To be loyal to God our Father is to love Him. To love Him is to honor His wishes. To honor Him is to obey Him. To obey

Him is to find ourselves enriched with the presence of His person. This is to be filled with His Spirit. This is to be empowered to live life to the fullest in quiet faith without fear of men or events.

This was precisely the case with Joshua. It was the unique quality of his character which, apart from Caleb, set him apart from all of his contemporaries. He was a soul utterly determined to serve God. Nothing would ever deter him from doing God's bidding no matter how absurd, unpopular or dangerous it might seem.

Out of the more than two million men and women who left Egypt en masse, only two devout, daring, obedient men and their families would ever enter Canaan forty years later. They were Joshua and Caleb, called upon now, with ten other companions, to go into the Promised Land to spy it out for Israel.

The people were now camped at a wilderness oasis called Paran. The name means "The Beautifying." It was on the border of the land promised so often by God to His people. Here was the occasion to enter into their inheritance. Here was the hour to vindicate the goodness of God who had delivered them from their enemies and brought them here in great might. Here the wilderness wandering could end and the beautiful bounties of a region flowing with milk and honey could begin.

All that Israel had to do was move in under God's great and generous hand. The land of promise lay stretched out before them. All that God asked was that they step out to take it over. Bit by bit, He would drive out and expel the inhabitants. Their part was simply to occupy the conquered territory as it was cleared before them.

But it was not to be!

Israel and Moses and Aaron had grave misgivings.

The mob instincts of doubt, skepticism and rank unbelief prevailed over the unflinching faith of the few.

The events of this cataclysmic occasion are recorded three times in God's Word. Once in the book of Numbers 13 and 14. Once in Deuteronomy 1, and again in Hebrews 3. To fully grasp what took place all three passages must be examined.

It becomes obvious that the Israelis insisted on first sending in spies to scout the terrain before they would dare to do God's bidding. They were so utterly persistent on this point that they prevailed upon Moses to comply with their own craven fears. In fact, their dark doubts and deliberate disbelief about God's intentions actually began to cloud Moses' own mind and changed his otherwise courageous conduct.

Capitulating to their demands, Moses chose one leader from each of the twelve tribes to serve as a special spy. Joshua, once called Oshea, the son of Nun, was selected from the tribe of Ephraim.

Under pressure from his perverse people, Moses gave them explicit instructions to determine whether or not Canaan was good or bad, wooded or open, fertile or barren, well-fortified or not, easy to conquer or difficult to overcome.

The audacity and flagrant presumption of such an assignment in the face of all God's previous promises utterly defies explanation. Again and again Jehovah had given His unequivocal assurance that the land of promise was a virtual paradise of plenty, whose complete occupation He would guarantee to Israel.

Yet rank disbelief had its day.

Tragic and terrible doubts distorted decisions.

Unbelief undid all that God had done.

The twelve spies slipped into Canaan quietly. They were away for forty days ranging widely over its tumbled terrain and verdant valleys. God allowed them to have their way.

When they returned they were bearing huge clusters of grapes so weighty and lush it took two men to lug them along.

Their reports were a commingled, confusing melange of contradictory facts. Their conflicting views were an absolute travesty of truth. In one breath they said all was beautiful, in the next all was terrible.

On one hand they declared emphatically it was in fact a region rich and fertile. Using explicit agricultural terminology they described it as being so productive it flowed with milk and honey. Its pastures were lush for their livestock, its fruits and crops abundant for their people.

Yet on the other hand they insisted it was such a desolate area it literally consumed its inhabitants, most of whom were outsize giants residing in great, high-walled cities.

In fact, all the ten spies, apart from Caleb and Joshua, insisted that they were so overwhelmed by the odds against them they felt as puny and helpless as the grasshoppers that clicked in the dry grass beneath their sandals. Only Caleb and Joshua were brave enough to believe Israel could move in and conquer the country at once.

But the two men were an unpopular minority.

In anger, bitterness and blind vituperation the crowd surged around Moses and Aaron charging them with duplicity and deception in bringing them to this dreadful place. All night they wept, wailed and murmured in rebellious agitation against God.

Blinded by their own unbelief, duped by their own self-deception and doubts, inflamed by their own fears and fantasies, the Israelis even demanded the appointment of a new leader and captain who would take them straight back into Egypt. They preferred to serve Pharaoh as slaves rather than follow God in freedom and triumph.

It was the hour of darkest degradation for Israel!

In utter terror Moses and Aaron flung themselves face down on the ground in craven subservience to the milling masses.

It seemed all was lost in the chaos and confusion.

But amid the turmoil God had two stalwarts.

Joshua and Caleb jumped to their feet, tore their tunics from them to gain the crowd's attention, then shouted to their countrymen fearlessly. What they said startled and enraged the people even further.

"The land to which God has brought us is an exceedingly good land! It is the Lord who can bring us into it if we but trust Him and please Him! It is God who can give us this region! It is He who will go with us if we obey Him! No need to fear, no need to fail! We can overcome!"

These are the sounds of a spirit attuned to God's Spirit. These are the sure trumpet notes of trust in the Almighty. These are the bugle blasts of the believer who sees with the pure perspective of faith in God and confidence in Christ.

But the angry masses, mad with hatred and blinded with rage, called for the blood of the two brave men. "Stone them with stones!" they shouted, ready to pick up rocks and hurl them with a vengeance.

At this precise point the majestic, overwhelming, awesome majesty of Jehovah's presence became apparent in the tabernacle. The effulgent glory of God overwhelmed the people. Suddenly all their stares were turned from Joshua and Caleb, Moses and Aaron, to see the splendor of God.

It was a perilous moment for Israel!

Her entire future as a nation hung by a hair!

In enormous indignation God declared to Moses that His patience with this provocative people had been exhausted. For a second time He expressed His desire to extinguish the rebellious rabble and initiate a new race with greater response to His will.

Again Moses interceded on behalf of his countrymen. Again he prevailed upon God to reconsider His intentions. Again he intervened to save Israel from immediate annihilation.

But what Moses could not do was avert ultimate judgment on their unbelief. Everyone of them except Joshua and Caleb, with their families, would only live to perish in this wretched wilderness. It was their own dreadful decision. Their graves would all be in this desperate desert—not one would enter Canaan.

4

Wasted Wilderness Years

FOR THE FOLLOWING awful forty years Israel was destined to wander in the desert wastes. It was an interlude of total impotence brought upon themselves by their unbelief, disobedience and rank rebellion against God.

It has been stated already in this book that it is an exceedingly dangerous thing to demand things from the Lord. Puny men sometimes treat the Almighty with grave contempt. They complain, find fault with His guidance, protest over His provision, and behave as though they know better than God Himself how to handle their affairs.

The astonishing and startling truth is that "God will give you what you grumble about." He will fulfill your wishes exactly according to your own words and your own faith (See Numbers 14:27–28). And this is why it is imperative to understand clearly what the consequences can be of your complaining.

In this case, all of Israel, except Joshua and Caleb, insisted God had only brought them into the wilderness to destroy them there. It was a false, contemptible charge. Yet it was an affront repeated again and again. They did not trust God, they only trusted their own deplorable wrong view of events. The end result was God granted them their own self-delusion and self-destruction. For they would simply go in circles, gaining no ground, until all their carcasses were consumed in this wretched wasteland.

For forty long, interminable years Joshua and Caleb with their quiet faith in Jehovah would have to endure the wanderings of their fellows. Yet the remarkable record of their own bright hope in the midst of such desolation enables us to see the sterling quality of their confidence in God. It was He who would sustain them in the interim. It was He who would preserve them to pass over Jordan into the land of promise. It was He who would enable them to conquer Canaan and find rest.

Because so many Christians, like Israel, spend years in the wilderness of wasted lives it is important to examine the reasons and causes in this chapter. Our basic unbelief, disobedience and rank rebellion against God are often not even noticed, much less understood, by those who claim to follow Christ, but really go nowhere with God.

It is with genuine compassion and a profound concern for others who may be wasting their years in pointless, empty wandering that I write these warnings. As an earnest lad of about ten I accepted the generous offer of God's salvation in Christ. I saw Him as my Savior, my deliverer from despair. Yet, for the next thirty years of my young life I lived very much for myself, wandering in the wilderness of divided loyalties, divided affections, divided interests, not willing to fully submit myself to His will as "Lord of my life." . . . "King of my will." . . .

The result was to wander in circles, so to speak, claiming to be Christ's follower, while in reality living largely for my own interests. It is a painful, pathetic path for anyone to tread. It leads nowhere except into the desert of despair. It ends only in ennui and cynicism. Nothing worthwhile is gained either for God or man. All is wasted.

Three basic causes lead to this condition. They are often tightly intertwined like a closely braided three-strand cord which binds us with unbreakable bondage. For purposes of simplicity and clarity I shall separate the three and deal with each individually.

Unbelief

In our highly sophisticated society, with its so-called civilized culture and higher education, we are taught to try, test and challenge every concept. We are urged to prove the reality of ideas, theories or hypotheses. Our mentors tell us to "discover the facts." We are encouraged to submit everything to the observable tests of our five fallible, fickle, physical senses in the scientific process.

Amid all of our proud and arrogant preoccupation with our human processes we completely omit and casually overlook the entire realm of the Spirit. Totally immersed in natural phenomena, we behave as though there were no supernatural forces at work in the universe. Utterly preoccupied with fallible human perspectives, we simply ignore God's view or His vision.

The net result is that we become people who are actually dominated and directed not by God, in whom we claim to believe, but by our own humanism based on:

1) Finding out facts.

2) Data processing.

3) Twentieth century technology—increasingly taking the form of computer print-outs, etc.

The consequence of such conduct is that we live our lives, not on the bedrock of fearless faith in God and His Word, but on the shaking sand of scientific fact-finding.

This is precisely what Moses and Israel did in sending spies into the Promised Land. Instead of simply trusting the Lord and acting on His advice, they decided to deliberately discover all the facts for themselves. It was utter folly. But beyond that it was blatant unbelief in God's commitments to them.

Following just facts leads one down a dangerous, slippery trail that can end only in failure. Here are the four fatal steps down to disaster:

1) Facts.
2) Fear.
3) Fantasy of foreboding.
4) Failure.

Invariably facts alarm people. Things always look so tough and difficult. This view gives rise to fear, doubt and misgivings. Then fantasies of foreboding take over. We are certain we cannot succeed. The end is failure and a flat refusal to carry out God's commands.

By examining the story of the spies carefully we see the exact parallels to this process at work in their experience. Rather than rely on God's assurance to them that He would bring them into a good land, a promised place of rest, they chose to find out all the facts for themselves first.

These immediately gave birth to formidable fears. They were preoccupied with the giants in Canaan, the high-walled cities they could not scale or conquer, the tough terrain they could not take.

Focusing on such fears led to terrifying fantasies. They appeared to themselves like wretched little grasshoppers. They could see nothing but disaster ahead. Their dark foreboding was death to any act of faith.

So they refused to go in to take the territory. Their mission was a total failure. They stood paralyzed and powerless. Not another step of progress could be taken because of their self-delusion and unbelief in the goodness of God.

We tend to look at Israel's conduct with scorn and contempt. We fault this ancient race for their folly and lack of faith. We are astonished by their fears and failures. Yet, the tragic truth is most of us still live our little "grasshopper lives" the same way. In cynical unbelief we go on wandering through our wilderness experience, not daring to trust Christ completely. We live with one foot trying to follow Him in fearless faith, the other foot moving back to find out all the facts. We fall between the two and accomplish nothing.

The church is often so deeply infiltrated by the world's mind-set on fact-finding that it has become utterly impotent. Christians unwittingly, unknowingly subscribe to humanistic technology and tactics to try and do God's work in the world. It simply does not function that way. We are to live by faith in God, not on the basis of observable facts around us!

Rebellion or Fault-finding

The second serious cause of wasted years in our walk with our Father is finding fault with His arrangement of our affairs. This attitude of human discontent with divine providence is referred to in God's Word by various names. Here are some of them: *rebellion, murmuring, fault-finding, being stiff-necked, provocation, discontentment, perverse attitudes.*

All of these terms are used to try to define the grievous grumbling of God's people. They represent our Father's devastating revelation of what many of us indulge in constantly. They really are synonyms for rank *self-pity.* And it will be recalled that in the opening chapter of this book the heinous nature of this sin against God was discussed.

Here I wish to discuss the root reasons for rebellion. If they are understood they can be grappled with effectively. But first we must see that murmuring and grumbling against God's care of us is the exact opposite to being grateful, thankful and genuinely appreciative of His arrangements.

This was Israel's horrible stance from the day of their Exodus from Egypt until the termination of their forty tragic years in the wilderness. They simply were never, ever satisfied as a people. They were forever critical of their God-given commander, Moses. They were always lusting and longing for something other than that provided for them. They were continually charging God with wicked motives designed to damage or destroy them.

Israel's favorite pastime was to find fault with their lot in life. They spent their miserable years moaning for the wretched conditions and grim slavery of Egypt. They were so quick to forget the remarkable miracles that had marked their desert sojourn, so slow to respond in gratitude to God's goodness, so eager to put the wrong interpretation on His intentions for them.

Many of us modern Christians are really no different. Our whole outlook on life is warped. We are bogged down by unbelief in the essential goodness of God. Our confidence in the impeccable character of Christ is tarnished and distorted by equating Him with our fallible human contemporaries. We assume His gracious Spirit is no more generous than our view of our grasping, greedy, human society.

In a word our entire view of our affairs is based on our erroneous human expertise and experience. We look out with the limited vision of our own unpredictability. We do not focus or fasten our attention on the thrilling faithfulness of our Father to us. We fail to look for His sure leading in our lives. We neglect to give Him hearty thanks for all His benefits bestowed on us.

The result is despair, not delight in His company.

What is even more deplorable is that amid our murmuring, criticism and complaining we actually prevent God from pouring out the benefits He would otherwise love to bestow upon us. We block His intentions toward us by our own inner intransigence. So we muddle along in a joyless, empty way that leads nowhere except to depression and despondency.

If our faith in God is to grow, it must be rooted in the ground of His formidable faithfulness to us. We must learn to look for His good intentions toward us as His own children. Then in genuine gratitude let us give thanks for all His arrangements of our affairs. Enormous blessings will follow.

Disobedience

So much has been written about deliberate disobedience to God (sin) that there is very little new here that can be said. Still it is pertinent to point out that because of rank disobedience to God's instructions, the Israelis who came out of Egypt never entered Canaan.

Not only did they grieve God, but they also deprived themselves of exciting conquests. They never took new territory. They never tasted the thrill of triumph over impossible obstacles. They never did enter into the rest intended for them. They were nothing but a helpless, deprived, forlorn people wandering hopelessly in the desert.

This is a desperate picture!

Yet, unhappily, it is true of too many of us today.

So we, too, must grasp the root cause of disobedience to our Father's good will for us.

First, and probably least understood, is our formidable human pride. As free persons we are free to choose whether or not we shall submit ourselves to God's wishes. In an act of reckless bravado we often flaunt His desires. We decide to "do our own thing" no matter how despicable. We act on our selfish impulses, not caring how others may be hurt by our harmful attitudes. Our main motive is self-assertion instead of seeking divine direction and submission to God's own gracious Spirit.

Second, we are often disobedient to our Lord's commands simply because we are afraid of failing in the attempt. We do not wish to "lose face." We do not wish to appear foolish to our associates. We do not want to step out boldly in following

Christ and so make a break with our culture, society or traditions. In other words we dare not be brave for God.

Third, disobedience is a clear revelation that we do not really know, love or honor God. If we did, we would not injure and offend Him with our obtuse behavior. Instead we would want, above everything else, to please Him by compliance with His commands. We would want to hearten and cheer Him with the faith of our obedience. We would bless Him with beautiful behavior based on a ready willingness to do His will.

How can all this begin to happen?

Capitulate completely to Christ. Invite Him to be Lord in your life! Give God the outright government of your affairs! Submit yourself swiftly to the sovereignty of His Spirit! Just do what He asks you to do (Philippians 2:13).

5

Joshua's Commission

THE FORTY DREADFUL YEARS in the desert had ground on remorselessly. The wilderness wastes took a steady toll of the Israelis. Year after year the corpses of mature men and women were buried in the burning sands of the Arabian hinterland. It was a time of terrible attrition for those who left Egypt in high hopes only to perish in the wilderness because of their perverseness.

Individuals who might have lived to achieve great exploits for God, simply sank into oblivion because of their opposition and disobedience to Jehovah's divine decrees for them.

Even Aaron the high priest died and his office was filled by his son Eleazer. Likewise with Moses, Israel's illustrious leader, the time had come for his departure from his people. Though still a virile man of undimmed vision at 120 years of age, his end had been decreed by the Almighty. He would be taken to a craggy mount from which he could get a broad overview of the land of promise. Yet, because of his own unbelief, the venerated leader would never be privileged to set his sandaled feet on its rich and fertile soil.

Instead of claiming and conquering Canaan, Moses would

have to be content with a pensive, distant view of what might have been his greatest glory. From the summit of Mount Abarim, meaning "the regions beyond," the old veteran looked with wistful longing at a land that would be taken in startling triumph by his successor.

To his unbounded credit, Moses did not choose or appoint the man to follow himself in the line of Israel's leadership. With resolute wisdom and keen spiritual perception he left this responsibility to God.

Moses no doubt recalled with crystal clear memory the momentous day before the burning bush when God had chosen, called, then commissioned him to be Israel's leader. Now he was equally anxious that his successor should be a man of God's own personal appointment. Only a man set over Israel by divine decree could ever hope to handle this difficult nation. It was an assignment far too onerous for any ordinary leader to assume.

"O God!" Moses implored. "You select the man. You set and establish him over this people. You send him in and out before them as supreme commander but also as a gentle shepherd."

It was a profound yet simple prayer.

And like most direct petitions made to God in utter earnestness it received a prompt reply.

The Lord's response was to instruct Moses to select Joshua, his trusted right hand man, in whom God's Spirit resided in abundant plenitude to be Israel's commander. It was he who should be commissioned to lead Israel henceforth. It was he who would take them across Jordan and into Canaan. It was he who by his fearless faith in God would triumph over the enemy, teaching Israel to obey the Lord. It was he who, at last, would enable Israel to find rest in the green pastures and beside the still waters of their promised inheritance.

It would be a tremendous turnaround for Israel. Instead of

tramping dejectedly in circles in the dusty old trails of despera-
tion in the desert, now they would begin to move into new
territory. Instead of blowing sand, burning rocks and scrub
thorn, they would cross Jordan into fields of grain and groves of
fruit. Instead of animal dung for fuel there would be forests of
trees to cut for firewood. Instead of flimsy tents they would
take over sturdy homes in strong cities with ample accom-
modation for all their families.

But all of this was possible only because of the caliber of man
chosen by God to lead His people. The sterling character of
Joshua, his dignified humility, his unshakable single-minded-
ness in serving Jehovah, his quiet, fearless faith in the Almighty, his intense sensitivity to God's Spirit, his courageous
willingness to be a man separated and obedient to God, set him
apart, head and shoulders above all his contemporaries, except
Caleb. He, too, was a choice individual destined to share in the
great victories that lay ahead.

There is, in all of this, very critical information for those
entrusted with finding suitable leaders for their congregations.
Far too often men and women assigned to select a new pastor
or minister for their church do not allow themselves to be
guided by God in their decisions.

There is an ever-increasing tendency in many groups to
decide upon a person's appointment either on the basis of
academic credentials or a pleasing personality. Some congregations place great emphasis upon a man's diplomas, degrees or scholastic attainments. Others appraise a candidate
upon the charisma of his conduct, the appeal of his personality
or the outer trappings of his temperament.

None of these is a sure criterion in the selection of a suitable
spiritual leader. As God spoke so pointedly to Samuel when he
went in search of a successor to King Saul, "The LORD seeth
not as man seeth; for man looketh on the outward appearance,
but the LORD looketh on the heart" (1 Samuel 16:7).

The heart of an individual is the will.

It is God who alone can discern the thoughts and innermost intents of a person's will.

It is the leader determined in his heart above all else to do God's will who can lead God's people into glorious triumph.

His main preoccupation is not to be popular.

His chief concern is not to play to his audience.

His only desire is to do God's will, and to lead His people to do likewise.

Joshua not only had a solemn responsibility and high honor to enter Canaan himself. He was entrusted with taking all his people in with him in total triumph.

No pastor, no spiritual leader, is ever able to take his people any further than he himself has gone with God. So ultimately the critical credential required of a spiritual elder is that he or she be indwelt and directed by the Spirit of the living God.

This was true in abundant measure of Joshua.

God Himself attested to this fact.

Subsequent successes would prove it.

And all the world was to see what a man of fearless faith could accomplish in company with God.

The instructions given by God for Joshua's commissioning as Israel's new commander-in-chief were surprisingly simple and brief. They lacked much of the pomp or pageantry often associated with the transfer of authority from an incumbent leader to his successor.

First, Moses was commanded to lay his hand on Joshua.

Second, he was to set him before Eleazer the priest in full view of all the people.

Third, he was to be given the solemn charge of leading Israel.

Fourth, to do this Moses would bestow on him the honor, prestige and authority of his office in order that Israel would obey.

Fifth, the High Priest would request of God, by means of URIM, wisdom and justice to command Israel with both courage and divine discernment.

Sixth, the High Priest would lay hands on him to give the spiritual charge of God.

And last, God would grant him divine wisdom to carry out His wishes.

In this straightforward way the supernatural "chain of command" from GOD → HIGH PRIEST → JOSHUA → ISRAEL, was clearly established for all to see.

Joshua was not a free-wheeling, flamboyant, self-asserting commander.

Rather, he was a man moving strongly, surely, as a spiritual leader under God's supreme authority. Herein lay part of the secret to his great success.

Combined with the role of military commander to his people Joshua also played the part of a pastoral shepherd tending the wayward flock of Israel. He recognized this solemn responsibility before God. Nor did he shrink from it. He knew full well that for Israel to please God it would take more than mere territorial conquests in Canaan.

He was a man of superb spiritual stature who realized Jehovah longed to take territory in the hearts and affections of His people. He desired to see Israel become obedient to His commands, and responsive to His will. His highest hope was that they become a separate people given to wholesome and righteous living.

For centuries to follow, the leaders who succeeded one another in the tempestuous history of this stubborn race would be a mixed lot. Some—like Gideon, Samuel, David and Hezekiah—would be great men of God indwelt by God's own Spirit as Joshua was. Others—like Ahab—would be corrupt and evil.

The tragic story of Israel was to be that of a people plundered by their own selfish, self-serving shepherds (see Ezekiel 34). It is always thus in the care of God's people. Even down to this very day there are still predators in the pulpits of many churches—those who seek only their own ends instead of the welfare of those under their care.

In Joshua's commissioning the rites of laying on of hands both by Moses and Eleazer were of special, solemn significance. This was much more than mere symbolism. It was the actual transfer of authority and power from God to the man of His particular appointment.

It is essential to understand that through the hand of Moses a measure of the authority, honor and power bestowed upon him by God, was, in turn being actually transferred now to Joshua. He would become a worthy successor, a brilliant military commander. The incredible conquests he would achieve would be not because of his personal genius but because of the power and presence of God's right hand guiding his decisions.

Joshua's fearless forays into enemy territory, his calm courage in the face of formidable obstacles, his intrepid strategy against the Canaanites would come directly from the majesty and might of the right hand of God Almighty upon him.

"Fear thou not; for I am with thee: be not dismayed; for I am thy God: I will strengthen thee; yea, I will help thee; yea, I will uphold thee with the right hand of my righteousness.

Behold, all they that were incensed against thee shall be ashamed and confounded: they shall be as nothing; and they that strive with thee shall perish.

Thou shalt seek them, and shalt not find them, even them that contended with thee: they that war against thee shall be as nothing, and as a thing of nought.

For I the lord thy God will hold thy right hand, saying unto thee, Fear not; I will help thee" (Isaiah 41:10–13).

Similarly through the hands of Eleazer the high priest there was bestowed on Joshua that spiritual dimension of divine wisdom, justice and keen perception without which he could not control Israel. It was imperative that he be endued with power from on high to govern and guide such an obdurate nation.

More than this, Joshua and Eleazer would be charged with partitioning the Promised Land among this people. It was an assignment so awesome most men would have recoiled from it. But empowered by God's Spirit, with His wondrous wisdom imparted to them in plenitude, this was a task undertaken without hesitation. Working in close cooperation, Joshua and Eleazer accomplished this decisive distribution of territory with outstanding success.

The record given to us of this momentous period in Joshua's career makes it clear that he was destined for great things because of his utter fidelity in "following the LORD" (see Numbers 32:10–12). No greater accolade could be bestowed upon a man under God than this.

In summary, "To follow the Lord" implied seven specific attitudes: 1) To love God and serve Him in total allegiance. 2) To be set apart at personal cost to serve God. 3) To relinquish one's own personal aims and ambitions for the welfare of others. 4) To play the part of a servant in ministering to God and His people. 5) To readily accept God's arrangements without question or complaining. 6) To gladly comply with His commands no matter how difficult or absurd they might seem. 7) To simply step out in fearless faith to do whatever God's will might be.

On the surface these seem simple and straightforward. In actual execution they demand the ultimate, total surrender of a man's will, emotions, mind and spirit to God. Because there are so few of us totally available to God's purposes in this way, seldom does His Spirit indwell a man or woman in such stupendous measure to become a formidable force in the world.

In the case of Joshua, God had found a man humble in heart,

singleminded in spirit, completely amenable to His control. The result was to so move upon Joshua that he became a literal "giant" in Israel.

His military genius, his spiritual stature were such that he was more than a match for the giants of Canaan who occupied their great, high-walled cities. Yet Joshua never indulged himself in self-adulation. He was wise enough and humble enough to recognize always that it was God's hand which gave him such signal success.

6

Joshua Receives Encouragement

IN HIS GRACIOUS CONCERN for Joshua, God arranged for him to be given enormous encouragement in assuming the leadership of Israel. Again and again he had seen the anguish, grief and frustration of Moses, his predecessor, in dealing with this difficult nation. He had been Moses' closest friend and associate during the terrible forty years of wasted wanderings in the desert.

Things would have to be different when he took over!

Joshua was not one who would stand for a replay of Israel's pathetic past.

It was time to take new territory, to gain fresh ground for God, to taste the fresh fruits of triumph.

But before all of this could happen it was imperative that he be given great encouragement in his assignment. The stirring spiritual support would come to him from three sources. First, it would be God, very God Himself, who would speak directly to His servant. Then there would be the good cheer and encouragement of Moses who, before his departure, would reassure Joshua of mighty victories to come. Finally, there was the steadfast counsel and spiritual insight of Eleazer the new high priest who would be his associate.

In this way it became clear to Joshua that without any doubt whatsoever he would take Israel into Canaan.

He was assured without a single misgiving that he and his people would occupy the land of promise. He was empowered to see, without any cloud of unbelief, that, beyond the Jordan, God would grant them rest from their enemies.

This sharp, bright vision of victories to come was never allowed to be dimmed or tarnished. The ultimate goal set before him by God of great things to come never faded. With fearless faith Joshua counted on God's commitments to him. This was the key to his future spectacular success.

When he did look back in retrospect, it was merely to remind himself of those remarkable times when Jehovah God had wrought such mighty miracles for Moses and Israel. From time to time he would recall the exciting Exodus from Egypt. He would relive momentarily the overthrow of Pharaoh's military might in the surging waters of the Red Sea. In his mind's eye he could recall his own first flush of victory over Amalek at Rephidim. He had clear, flashing memories of the defeat of Sihon, king of the Amorites, and Og, king of Bashan.

The Lord had been faithful to him. He had demonstrated His might. He had made strong His arm on behalf of His people.

If He could do it before, He could do it again—and again!

Joshua had learned the great spiritual principle that the surest way to increase one's faith in God is to concentrate one's attention upon the utter faithfulness of God. To do this is to dispel the fear and foreboding from one's own view. His focus was centered, not on the formidable obstacles that lay ahead, but on the utter trustworthiness of the Lord Himself.

Over and over the word of encouragement which came to Joshua was simple yet startling. "It is God who shall go before you! It is God who shall fight for you! It is God who, little by little, shall steadily and surely give you victory over the enemy! It is God who shall eventually give you rest!"

This was strong meat for a man of unshakable confidence in his God. He understood clearly that his call to action came from the Most High. Yet at the same time he understood positively that the power to carry out that commission was not in himself but in the dynamic presence of the Living God who accompanied him.

To put it succintly in the language of the New Testament, "It is God which worketh in you both to will and to do of his good pleasure" (Philippians 2:13).

Joshua was encouraged to see that his assignment from God was not exclusively his, but it was a commissioning for combat and conquest that was of divine dimensions. He came to grasp, better than Moses ever did, the idea that it was essentially God's work, God's will, God's way that was being achieved in company with God.

Moses repeatedly expressed the feeling that he alone bore the burden of governing Israel. He asked for relief and respite from the crushing load of leading such a stubborn nation. He seemed shattered by the strain of more or less "going it alone."

No doubt this had often troubled his young lieutenant, Joshua. So now it was imperative for this new and younger commander to have a different perspective. He must somehow see clearly that he was not alone. Rather, it was God and he together who would achieve great triumphs. It was God and he who would lead Israel into exciting achievements. It was God and he in close cooperation who would occupy Canaan.

All of this was possible, not because Joshua was a great genius, but because he moved in intimate communion with a great God, whom he trusted implicitly.

It was to this end and for this purpose that just at the end of his career Moses challenged Joshua to present himself to the Lord for service.

The word "present" carries with it enormous implications. It combines within it the dual concept of offering oneself in total allegiance to another of higher and more noble rank. It is also at heart a military term meaning that one is utterly expendable on behalf of the commander (Deuteronomy 31:14–23).

This is the same special service which Paul urged upon the Christians at Rome when in stirring, challenging language he wrote so forcibly: "I beseech you therefore, brethren, by the mercies of God, that ye present your bodies a living sacrifice (expendable), holy, acceptable unto God, which is your reasonable service" (Romans 12:1).

This Joshua did promptly without hesitation or delay.

He was not a man, like Moses, who offered up a string of excuses for not carrying out God's commands.

He saw his responsibility to God and to Israel with intense integrity to carry out his commission from on high.

He understood emphatically what his duties were.

He had his marching orders from God. He would go!

This total, unquestioning availability to the purposes of the Lord was the second great key to his brilliant career.

In response to his readiness to present himself totally to God, he was endowed with a supernatural infilling of divine wisdom by the Spirit of God (Deuteronomy 34:9 and Acts 5:32).

Not only had he been called and commissioned as Israel's supreme commander, now he was encouraged to carry out his special assignment with God's unique spiritual anointing upon his life. He was a general filled with the Spirit of God . . . wise beyond any of his contemporaries.

The result was not only would he do God's bidding, but so, too, would all of Israel under his command.

What a triumph!

As long as Moses held prior position in Israel, it was as though Joshua waited patiently in the wings, ready to step on center stage as soon as his predecessor had played his part and bowed out. This now took place. Moses was called aside by

God to die on the wild mountains east of Jordan. There only
God knew where he would be buried.

The long, tedious wilderness days were at an end.

The change of command had come.

And now Jehovah addressed Joshua directly (see Joshua 1).

In clear-cut, concise commands, the specific steps which
would lead to Joshua's spectacular success were given to him.
By carrying them out, this new commander would achieve in a
few weeks what Moses could not accomplish with Israel in forty
years of frustration.

This mandate for conquest and victory stands as one of the
most heroic and valid statements of divine decree in all of the
Old Testament Scriptures. It represents the absolute authority
of God delivered to man for triumph over evil. Its content is as
applicable to the Christian today as it was to Israel 3400 years
ago. We do well to examine it carefully.

Any person who has a burning desire to move from an empty, pointless life of wandering in the wilderness of divided
loyalties, to triumph under Christ's control, will find the formula here. There are specific steps to take:

1) The individual must be humble in heart, meek in spirit,
easily entreated of the Lord. Throughout his quiet years of long
service to Moses, Joshua had shown these attributes and
attitudes.

God delights to draw near and commune with a man contrite
in his behavior. It is the humble soul who of necessity must
exercise faith in God who is greater than himself. It is he whom
the Lord honors. It is he who is elevated to new responsibilities
and exciting conquest.

2) The word of the Most High to this person is: *"Arise—go
over!"* This is a categorical command that implies an immediate, positive response. In layman's language it means: *"Get up
and get going!"*

This was a phrase used by Christ again and again in His

contact with his contemporaries. It demanded an act of the will on the part of the one addressed. It called for action!

The days of drifting around aimlessly in the desert were done. The time to get up and move forward under God's guidance was here: no more vacillation; no more debating the issue.

3) One's attention and aims had to be refocused on God's aims and ambitions. It was no longer a question of what Israel's petty preferences might be. Rather it was a case of moving out to accomplish God's purposes and plans. His aim was to give them the enemy-held land, to give them the taste of conquest, to find the place of rest and peace.

4) These tremendous achievements would not be accomplished in a day or two. They were not attained in a single spectacular leap of victory. Instead, it would be a steady march forward one day at a time, one step at a time, little by little, until all the territory was taken.

Too many Christians want instant results. They look for an overnight metamorphosis. They are conditioned to believe they can become conquerors in a week-end crash course of spiritual seminars. Not so!

God's clear communique to Joshua was simple and sure. *"Every place that the sole of your foot shall tread upon, that have I given you!"* Our role is to step out in faith and claim quietly our rightful inheritance given to us in Christ. This is to take territory with God—a bit every day!

5) The land promised to Joshua and Israel was not just some narrow strip along the Jordan valley. It was a wide, immense region stretching from the Negev desert in the south to Lebanon in the north, from the Euphrates in the east, to the shining Mediterranean Sea in the west.

Likewise, God's aspirations for us are enormous, often beyond our wildest dreams—not because we are great people, but because He is a great God, who delights to do great things with us.

6) The special encouragement given to Joshua was that his foes could not prevail against him. Because it was God who would not fail him, who would not forsake him.

His confidence was not in himself but in Jehovah.

So with us! We are not encouraged by our self-confidence or self-reliance. Rather, our confidence reposes in the great strong character of Christ and His commitments to us. Our sufficiency in the struggle is found in the grandeur of our God.

7) In order for Joshua to be victorious it was imperative that he and all of his people comply carefully with the commands and ordinances of God. These were not onerous, weighty e-dicts designed by deity to suppress Israel. Quite the contrary, they were the divine arrangements of God for the full-orbed well-being of His people. Obey them and they would prosper! Ignore them and they would perish!

It was not a question of legalism but of loyalty and love to the Lord. And Christ Himself made it abundantly clear over and over that to love Him was to obey His commands and comply with His wishes (John 14, 15, 16).

8) Joshua was given to understand emphatically that as the Word of God became the supreme center of his concern he was bound to prosper—bound to conquer, to enjoy enormous success.

We simply cannot overexpose ourselves to the Scriptures. They must become the central core of all our convictions as Christians. God's Word reveals to us in unmistakable terms what His will and wishes are. The responsibility for reading His instructions lies with us. The carrying out of His com-mands rests with us. The positive response of our wills to His will depends upon us and our total availability to His purposes. His Word can become to us Spirit and life!

The instant God detects in us the faintest intention to com-ply with His supreme desires, He immediately moves into our lives and experience to energize us in the joint exercise. It is

He who provides the power, the courage, the capacity to conquer. As Paul put it so well, "That he would grant you, according to the riches of his glory, to be strengthened with might by his Spirit in the inner man; that Christ may dwell in your hearts by faith; that ye, being rooted and grounded in love, may be able to comprehend with all saints what is the breadth, and length, and depth, and height; and to know the love of Christ, which passeth knowledge, that ye might be filled with all the fulness of God.

"Now unto him that is able to do exceeding abundantly above all that we ask or think, according to the power that worketh in us, unto him be glory in the church by Christ Jesus throughout all ages, world without end. Amen" (Ephesians 3:16–21).

In fearless faith Joshua grasped all that God had said to him for his personal encouragement. He saw vividly the steps to success and heart-pounding victories.

Without fanfare or theatrics he in turn took his first calm step of faith in God. He issued this simple direction to Israel: *"Prepare rations—within three days you will pass over Jordan to go in and possess the Promised Land!"* (see Joshua 1:11).

He was ready to move mightily with God. In a few days he did what Moses failed to achieve in forty years!

7

Reconnoitering Jericho

DURING THE BUSY three days before the heroic and unforgettable crossing of the Jordan, Joshua felt constrained of God's Spirit to make two significant moves. The first was to challenge the three tribes of Israel which had elected to live east of the river to fulfill their pledge to Moses in sending their armed men across the flooding Jordan for conquest. The second was to send a pair of undercover agents into Canaan to reconnoiter Jericho in preparation for attack.

Approximately a year previous to this, the three tribes of Reuben, Gad and Manasseh had approached Moses to request permission to settle in the rugged rangeland east of the Jordan. They were the leading livestock men of Israel. The open grasslands and semi-desert terrain were ideal for sheep and cattle. In fact, their initial desire was to immediately occupy this rather difficult region and there establish their homes, corrals and livestock operations. Moses, at first, was rather reluctant to agree to such an arrangement, but finally conceded that it could be done but only on one condition. Reuben, Gad and the half tribe of Manasseh who remained east of Jordan would have to send their fierce warriors across Jordan with the rest of Israel to assist in the conquest of Canaan. This they agreed to do. And it was this commitment to which Joshua now called them. Their fighting men would form the advance guard for Israel.

In years to come these three tribes would regret that their forbears had been content to settle on the desert side of Jordan. Their descendents would eventually be the first to fall into enemy hands and be made slaves to the Assyrians who invaded and conquered them (1 Chronicles 5:25–36). But even long before this, these self-satisfied people would have disturbing heart-searchings over the failure of their forefathers to enter and live in Canaan.

The profound spiritual principle at work here, applies always to God's people. We are given the free-will choice to decide for ourselves at what level of spiritual attainment we shall live in our walk with God. We can walk in the wilderness of divided loyalties and divided affections until the day we die. We can settle down cosily just a short way from the life of conquest and victory to be content with only a distant view of our inheritance in Christ. Or with courage, faith and joy in the Lord we can enter fully into the victory and rest intended for us by our Father.

Joshua, bold and wise leader that he was, immediately reminded these tribes of their vows to God and their serious obligations to fight side by side with their brothers in battle. He was not a commander who would permit some of the people to relinquish their responsibilities at great risk to their fellows. It was a classic demonstration of his determination to see that God's will would be carried out in proper order, even at considerable cost and inconvenience to those concerned.

Some of the warriors from Reuben, Gad and the half tribe of Manasseh would be away from their wives, families, homes and herds for weeks and months at a stretch. This separation would be a painful ordeal that lasted for years until at last all of Israel found rest from its foes. Everything has its price! And the person who refuses to become a full-orbed overcomer for Christ soon finds there is a great cost to compromise.

To be out of the center of God's will is to be on the eccentric periphery of His best purposes. There the rub and abrasion of knowing one has missed His best intentions, living in sad mediocrity, gives the reluctant soul sorrow and despair. These are the "half-way people," these are the "half-hearted warriors," these are the carnal Christians.

Having clearly settled this issue with the three tribes, Joshua now turned his attention to Jericho. It was the closest, large, high-walled city lying across Jordan. He was determined to storm its walls and take it captive in a brilliant first assault.

In blazing contrast to the weak-kneed, indecisive, vacillating mission arranged by Moses forty years before to spy out the land with twelve spies, Joshua acted now in fearless faith. For forty long, tedious, trying years he had waited quietly for this momentous opportunity. For what to him had seemed like an endless eternity he longed to step out and lead Israel to triumph in bold moves of power.

Fearlessly he and Caleb had declared forty years before that the Canaanites were "but bread" for the hosts of Israel to consume. He had dared to stand in peril of his life and shout that God Himself would give them this fierce territory. Now he was taking the first step of fearless faith in claiming the ground God had given.

Joshua's two emissaries were now to be the very first to ford the flooding river. They were the first to set foot within enemy territory. They were the first to tread upon the turreted walls of Jericho's ramparts. And every place their feet were set upon was ground guaranteed to them by God. They were not on a fact-finding mission. They were simply having a preview of victory. The report they brought back would not be a mixed bag of disturbing data. It would, instead, be a clear picture of complete conquest under the mighty hand of God.

When the two men infiltrated Jericho their first contact was Rahab, a beautiful young woman, a harlot by profession. She could be immediately identified by her unveiled head and face. Prostitutes boldly revealed their beauty in this way. Men could appraise their charms and attractiveness with a fleeting glance from the street.

For the two undercover agents, entry into a harlot's establishment would arouse a minimum of suspicion from the local residents. And because her home was on the outer wall, they had identified her premises before ever they passed through the gates. For she had been seen looking out a window . . . the same window through which later they would escape.

Long, long before ever the two men met Rahab, the very Spirit of the Living God had been within those high walls. He had moved upon the mind and emotions of this young woman. He had, through the events, rumors and random reports of God's dealing with Israel, influenced the will of this lady. No doubt various travelers crossing the Middle East from Egypt to Arabia and back, had made overnight stops at her establishment. All of them shared with her the heart-stirring accounts of Israel's Exodus from Egypt. They told of Israel's sojourn in the desert, sustained in wondrous and miraculous ways by Jehovah. They described Israel's victories over Sihon, king of the Amorites and Og, king of Bashan.

For Rahab it was really only a matter of time until total destruction would overtake her own city of Jericho. She had no way of being sure exactly when the overthrow would come. But in the midst of all her fear and apprehension there began to germinate a seed of faith that somehow, in some remarkable way, unknown to her, both she and her family could be preserved amid the holocaust. Her confidence reposed not in her own meager resources as a reprobate member of a pagan society, but rather in the greatness of Israel's God.

So when the two young Israelis entered her quarters, she knew with a profound inner conviction, prompted by God's Spirit, that they were not there to enjoy her company. They were there to prepare her for the crisis hour in her career.

Her conversation immediately turned to those matters which were uppermost in her mind. She *knew* assuredly that her country would be conquered by Israel. By her own testimony she gave voice to the truth that the God of Israel had given Israel both this city and the surrounding territory. Because of such an awareness all the Canaanites lived in terror of the impending invasion.

In view of all this Rahab had complete confidence that only by entrusting herself to Jehovah God could she be spared. Only in Him was there salvation for herself and her family.

She and her house were obviously under careful surveillance by the king of Jericho. Soon after the two foreigners had entered her premises, word was brought to him of their arrival. He immediately sent word that the strangers be brought to him for interrogation.

Crafty and cunning woman that she was, Rahab was not to be taken unawares. She had been fully prepared for such an emergency. With her quick wit and sharp intelligence she had escorted them to the roof of her home and hidden them under the long-stemmed stalks of flax spread up there in the sun to cure.

When palace guards arrived to arrest the two spies, Rahab, still steeped in her old pagan ways, which revelled in deception, assured the investigators that her guests had long since left, probably for the Jordan fords. At least that was the direction in which the king's officials went in search of them.

Rahab, in providing protection for the two young Israelis with the covering of flax, had made a memorable move of enormous spiritual significance. It was from the long flexible fibers of the flax that linen was made. The use of linen in the apparel of the priests always stood for the righteousness of God. The linen ephod and the linen garments spoke of the purity and protection of the Most High. Only garbed in linen did any man dare to enter the Holy of Holies to meet the God of Israel before the mercy seat of the ark of the covenant.

The flax used to make the strong, beautiful linen was also spun and braided into strong rope—the very rope by which Rahab would provide an escape for the two men through her window on the wall. It was the same red-dyed rope which would dangle from that outer window to guarantee security for her and her family during the invasion by Israel.

Whether knowingly or not, Rahab, with a deep intuition of spiritual insight, was demonstrating by her action that her total reliance was grounded upon the "righteousness of another." Her hope of salvation rested upon the justice of the Lord God of Israel. She invested her confidence in the assurance given to her that it was under the protection of the "red rope" she and her family would be spared, just as previously the spies had been saved under the flaxen fibers spread over them on the roof of her home.

It was this action of implicit, viable, living faith in the mercy and justice of God that gave her redemption. It was exactly akin to the blood of the Passover lamb sprinkled on the lintel and door posts of Israeli homes in Egypt. Such a sign guaranteed the survival of the occupants who that night would not only be "passed over" by the destroying angel, but also would "pass over" out of Egypt and its slavery, into a new life of freedom under God.

Rahab exercised remarkable confidence in the covenant of God's messengers for herself, but even more so for her entire family who would be rescued from the ruins of Jericho. Because of such formidable faith, this pagan prostitute would in due time be brought into the very warp and woof of the life of Israel. She would be taken as a legitimate wife by Salmon. Her son would be called Boaz, who later married Ruth. And thus she was to become the great, great grandmother of David, Israel's greatest king. What a signal honor, recorded so carefully in the New Testament genealogies (Matthew 1:5–6)!

That first evening, after her conversation with the two young Israelis, under cover of darkness she let them down over the city wall on her red rope. Skillfully she instructed them to flee to the high country away from Jordan. There they would hide out for three days. When the coast was clear, and their pursuers had returned to Jericho, they could recross the Jordan back to their own camp in safety.

All of these heart-warming events were a profound prefiguring of the great salvation provided to all men and women who would put their trust in Christ. It was a divine foreshadowing of the laid-down life of God, poured out in His shed blood and broken body on Calvary—the supreme sacrifice of "The Righteous One" who was made to be sin for us that we, in turn, would be made right with His righteousness.

This was the redemption of a just and righteous God which Rahab seized. It was the act of obedient, living faith which transformed her from her past as a pagan prostitute, to an esteemed and cherished mother in Israel.

As for Joshua's two undercover agents, who had survived under cover of the linen fibers, they returned to their commander at the end of three days in the high country. Their full report of what transpired within Jericho's walls was a thrilling tale. It stirred Joshua to the depths. His resolve to cross Jordan the next day was reinforced by the exciting good news.

"Yes," the two eager warriors reassured their leader, "truly God, very God, has delivered all the land of Canaan into our hands!" They grinned happily at the thought. "All the enemy is faint and fearful at the thought of our invasion!"

It was exactly the encouragement Joshua needed on this last night before his forces approached the flooding Jordan the next day. It was the magnificent provision arranged by God to fortify his faith on the eve of the great invasion. The next day Israel would break camp for the last time in their forty years of hopeless wilderness wanderings.

The Exodus from the desert was about to begin!

The new trek of triumph with God would be underway!

From endless vacillation Israel now would enter an era of victory!

8

Joshua Crosses Jordan

LONG BEFORE the red dawn had streaked the eastern sky Joshua arose in his tent. The day to pass over Jordan had come. Excitedly but quietly Israel's new commander communed with his God. Earnestly Joshua besought Jehovah for courage, wisdom and sure guidance.

He was but one man among the millions of his fellow countrymen. But he was one man who truly knew the Lord. He was one man who exulted in the awareness that the forty frustrating years of wilderness wanderings were over and the conquest of Canaan was just ahead.

Clear and concise direction had come to him on how the people under his command should march. This was not to be a haphazard movement executed without any specific order or regulation. Quite the opposite! The entire mass of over two million persons would proceed under very definite guidelines.

First of all messengers, officers under direct instructions from Joshua, had already been dispatched to each tribe. They were instructed to focus their attention on the ark of the covenant of God. This sacred chest, overlaid with gold and surmounted by the mercy seat between its wondrous cherubim, would lead the march. It was borne aloft on the broad, strong shoulders of the priests drawn from the tribe of Levi.

This sacred ark, so long sheltered within the inner sanctum of the Holy Place in the tabernacle, would now be lifted up to full view. All of Israel must clearly understand that where it led they must follow.

The ark contained within it the sacred tablets of stone bearing the Ten Commandments carved on them by the finger of God. It held Aaron's rod that had budded. It bore a bowl of the manna which had been Israel's staple food for forty years. But most important it bore all the law of God, delivered and recorded by Moses (Deuteronomy 31:26).

In essence, and in fact, the ark bespoke the very Presence of God among His people. It was in it and through it that God met with them through the high priest. The ark represented all the covenant promises made by God to His people. More than even that, however, it stood for the power and might of the Almighty to enable Israel to carry out the commandments of God.

As the ark moved, so they were to move. As the ark broke new ground, they were to break new ground. As the ark was taken into the flooding current of the Jordan, so they were to advance fearlessly into the formidable future.

Very deliberately Israel was instructed that no one was to crowd up close to the sacred chest of the Most High. A distance of roughly one thousand yards should separate the priests who bore it and their associates. It was to be held in high esteem. It was to be clearly visible for all to see it, even those at a distance. It was to be the absolute center of attention for all who followed in its train.

Here, in the unique and unlikely ways of God, was a nation moving into battle, launching an invasion of historic magnitude without the blaring of bugles or sound of battle cries. This was no ordinary taking of territory in the tradition of an army on the attack. This was the mass movement of a people under divine direction.

Joshua made it abundantly clear that for Israel this was a brand new maneuver. For this nation, this was a way that they had never been over before. They were starting to move with implicit faith in God. What He said they would do. Where He led they would follow. Only in this way would or could they ever know exactly what His intentions were for them.

It was the ark of the covenant which would lead the people. It was the ark of the Lord which would command the flood. It was the ark of Promise which would enable them to prevail over the Promised Land.

The lessons for us as God's people in the closing years of the twentieth century are as vital and applicable as in Joshua's time. It is important that we pause here to grasp and understand the basic principles underlying the life of faith in God.

If we are to move forward in our walk with the Lord, it becomes possible only as we are guided by God. This is fairly simple to state on paper in so many words. Yet in actual practice it becomes difficult to do unless we give our implicit obedience to the Word of God.

Just as Joshua insisted that it was the ark of God, containing the laws of the Lord which were to determine Israel's direction, so with us and the Word of God. It simply must become our guide in life. The Scriptures must be to us much more than a mere book. They must become the standard borne aloft to which we look for direction in every move we make. The "words of the Almighty" must be both life and spirit which energize, sustain and propel us forward into formidable situations.

Putting it into plain language we must, as God's people, come to the place where we have enormous confidence in God's covenant with us. It is He who has made His own generous commitments to us. It is He who guarantees us victory over the vicissitudes of life, who assures us of fruitfulness instead of fear, who in His own wondrous ways will give us rest amid the turmoil of our times.

Yet, we have our part to play in all of this. Joshua was to point out this fact to his people again and again. There would be times to move when the ark moved. There would be times to stand still when the ark stood still. Our response always must be one of prompt and hearty cooperation with the commands of God's Word.

We do not debate the issue with the Lord. We simply comply. This calls for undeviating devotion to the disclosed will of Christ. It calls for constant exposure to His commands so that we are familiar and in harmony with His intentions. It calls for our readiness to respond in energetic and eager cooperation.

For all of us there are bound to be formidable "floods" in the stream of life. Just as Joshua and Israel now faced a raging river that overflowed its banks and inundated its flood plain, so will we. God does not try to hold us back from the rampaging currents of life. He does not ask us to retreat or withdraw from that threat which would seem to engulf us. He does not urge us to try and find some way around the apparently impossible barriers before us. Rather He asks us to believe quietly that:

It is He who brought us here.

It is He who will keep and preserve us here.

It is He who will take us on from here.

This is faith in action. This is the private, positive response of the person whose confidence reposes in Christ. This is the inner attitude of will and spirit of the individual who experiences great advances with God.

For ultimately it is the Lord who shows Himself strong on behalf of those who will without fear or foreboding quietly step out into the surging streams of life. There they will see what great wonders God can perform. They never happen if we hold back on the riverbank waiting for the dry weather season to come.

Joshua knew that all of Israel had to see these first faltering

steps vindicated by God. He realized that it was utterly imperative they be prepared to set foot in the rushing, muddy waters
as a deliberate act of faith. This was to set down the soles of
their feet in an impossible situation claiming the ground in
faith. Then, and only then, would they see the intervention of
the Most High in holding back the flood so they could cross
over the river bottom on dry ground.

But before ever this could occur the nation had to sanctify
itself, cleanse its conscience, purify its motives.

This momentous historical occasion was not an event to
honor Israel. It was a pivotal point to prove to all people of all
time that the Lord God is all-powerful, totally trustworthy in
even the most impossible places.

The particular word of encouragement given to Joshua from
God just here was very reassuring to the new commander. Just
as the prestige and honor of Moses was established in Israel
when they crossed the Red Sea, now in a similar way Joshua's
leadership and preeminence would be confirmed in crossing
Jordan. Never again would there be any doubt as to his divine
appointment.

This was essential if Joshua was to be respected, honored
and obeyed by this obdurate nation. His leadership was not an
office seized by self-assertion. It was an assignment of noble
design arranged by God. For in Joshua He had found a man of
fearless faith.

That formidable quality in his character made it possible for
Joshua to order the priests bearing the ark to simply step right
into the surging waters of the flood. What to his associates
might have seemed like an impossible situation, was to Joshua
but the opportunity for Jehovah "to provide a way where there
was no way."

Joshua did not focus on the flood. He did not allow himself to
become preoccupied with the problem of providing his people
with a passage. He did not allow his attention on the ark to be
distracted by other diversionary doubts.

His instructions to his people were plain and to the point. "Set your feet right in the river. Step right into the flood without fear. Stand still in the swirling current that surges around you. Steadfastly see that God, very God, has gone before you into this Jordan. Surely the waters will assuage south of you, giving dry ground on which to cross, while to the north the river is held back in its valley by the mighty hand of God."

These were not the wild, fanatical fantasies of a charlatan. This was not the empty bravado of a self-deluded impostor. This was not the crowd manipulation of a "would-be God." Rather here was a man of quiet, serene faith in God, counting upon the Almighty to provide His people with a path through the impossible place.

Isaiah, the prophet of the Lord, some 750 years later in the history of Israel, reiterated exactly the same profound and stirring conviction:

"So shall they fear the name of the LORD from the west, and his glory from the rising of the sun. When the enemy shall come in like a flood, the spirit of the LORD shall lift up a standard against him" (Isaiah 59:19).

In whole-hearted response to Joshua's fearless faith in God, not only the priests bearing the ark, but also all of Israel broke camp as one man. Without hesitation or debate, much less complaining or fault-finding, they folded their tents for a last time in the wilderness. With their goods and victuals, children, livestock and long-worn clothing they moved en masse toward the river.

Bravely, boldly, without foreboding, the vanguard of the priests, the ark high on their shoulders, stepped into the murky, muddy waters of the racing river. The swirling current charged with silt eddied momentarily about their ankles. But quickly the water level began to subside around their feet.

Unafraid, unabashed, the priests stood quietly in place. To their delight the waters south of them drained away to expose the river bed. To the north, the flood backed up the valley spilling out over the flood plain. Under the fierce heat of the Mideastern sun the silt of the river bottom quickly dried, providing wide, safe passage for the masses of people and their herds of livestock.

All of Israel, as well as Joshua, Caleb and their immediate families, gained new ground on the other side. Their first camp in Canaan would be on the banks of the river immediately in front of Jericho. It had been a momentous day in Israel's unhappy history. It was an hour of total triumph in which God had shown His power on their behalf.

In a remarkable and reassuring way, Jehovah had again shown His chosen people that His commitments to them were utterly reliable. It was His specific promise to Joshua that every place they put down their feet to possess He would give to them. Even in the midst of the flooding river they set down their soles and were granted ground for safe passage.

Here was a classic demonstration to all men of all time that when they move out of their tents of ease and comfort to take new steps of faith in Christ, tremendous things happen. It was a historic event demonstrating the remarkable results achieved when God and man cooperate. It was He who had preserved, sustained and brought Israel to this point. It was God who held back the flood waters. It was He who provided safe passage for all Israel into the Land of Promise.

Yet it was the Israelis who had to be willing, on their part, to pack up their tents, break camp, move out of their safe security and set their feet in the flooding river.

The spiritual principle here is potent for God's people, even today. The questions we must ask ourselves are searching. "Am I prepared to move out of my little tent of personal security to follow Christ?" "Perhaps most of my life has been spent taking care of my 'tent' of safety. Maybe my friends, my family, my profession, my assets, my cozy location in life, my career, my familiar, comfortable arrangements have restricted me from moving out boldly to take new and daring steps in doing God's will."

Second, if I am prepared to pack up and move out of the old wearisome wilderness, "Will I unflinchingly set my feet down in the most formidable place, fully expecting my Lord to hold back the flood that threatens me?"

It is the person who does this with calm trust in the integrity of Christ who finds Him totally trustworthy. He does perform wonders on our behalf. He does provide a way through impossible situations. He does enable us to triumph and take new territory.

Try Him and discover new ground with God!

9

The Jordan Memorials

NOT ONLY WAS the crossing of Jordan a stirring event for Israel, but also a terrifying development for all of the Canaanite tribes west of the river. As the hordes of men and women streamed across the valley bottom bearing their tents, tiny infants and household effects, cold fear gripped the minds of their future foes.

This was the fearsome invasion of their territory which they had dreaded for a full forty years. The armed men of Israel were setting foot on their soil. A massive initial bridgehead was established on the low plains before Jericho. This first encampment in Canaan would be aptly named Gilgal, meaning "My reproach is removed."

At last, at long last, after all their wearisome, dreary wanderings in the desert, this nation under God's hand and Joshua's command, was on the move for Jehovah. It was a day of jubilation, an hour of triumph, a monumental memorial to the honor of God Himself. Here the ominous reproach and shameful record of Israel's wretched intransigence was erased.

Amid all the excitement and enthusiasm God spoke clearly to Joshua about the erection of a suitable memorial at Gilgal to commemorate the crossing. For in truth this was as new and fresh a triumph for Israel now, as the crossing of the Red Sea in their Exodus from Egypt had been exactly forty years before. It was the dawn of a great beginning in a new land under a new command.

Israel's days of sullenly refusing to respond to the guidance of God under Moses were gone. Their wretched complaining at the commands of the Almighty was ended. The desperate, hopeless wanderings in the wilderness of their own divided minds and emotions were now behind them. Their self-pity, self-gratification were past. They were a people with a powerful purpose, determined now to take territory with God.

Likewise for the Christian there are those monumental occasions which stand out with startling clarity in his/her walk with God. There is the initial hour of deliverance from our slavery to sin and Satan, the enemy of our souls. That point of "passing-over" from death to life, from darkness to light just as surely as Israel on the night of its first Passover feast escaped from servitude and slavery in Egypt to freedom under God across the Red Sea.

Unfortunately and unhappily for most of us, as with Israel, there then follow forlorn years of wandering in the wilderness of divided minds, divided affections, divided loyalties. On the one hand we do desire to follow Christ, to comply with His commands, yet, sad to say, on the other hand we still hanker for the former low life style of "Egypt." The world is very much with us. We are tantalized by its attractions, titillated by its tempting desires. Our wills are not yet made totally available to the powerful purposes of God Almighty. So in despair and despondency we stumble around in circles, going nowhere, achieving little, people of split personalities.

We claim to be Christians. We call ourselves the children of God. We insist we are following Christ. In reality, we are all the time serving ourselves and living in defeat and despair as carnal, worldly-minded individuals.

Ultimately, as with Israel, the day dawns when there comes

an end to the dismal old self-life of despair and discouragement. In an act of bold faith in God we decide to abandon
ourselves and capitulate completely to Christ. We give over
the government of our lives to God Himself. We submit our
wills deliberately to the sovereignty of His Spirit. Then in
implicit, unquestioning obedience we step out to comply with
His wishes.

This is a titanic pivot point in any person's walk with God.
This is the crossing of the Jordan. This is, if you will, the
crossing of the Rubicon, for the Christian. From then on there
is no looking back. There is no returning to the weary old
wilderness days of the wretched desert years.

We are moving onto new ground with God. This deserves
and demands a bold memorial.

Joshua's instructions from the Lord were very explicit. He
would select one man as a representative from each of the
twelve tribes of Israel. These sturdy fellows were each to pick
up a rock from the river bed where the priests stood who
carried the ark of God. These twelve special stones upon which
the feet of the priests had trodden, would be carried across to
the far west bank of the Jordan. There, in their rough, uncut,
unchiselled, natural condition Joshua would erect them in
three tiers of four stones each as a permanent memorial in the
sight of all the nation.

Those twelve rough rocks represented to all men of all time
two strategic and signal principles in the horrendous history of
Israel. First and foremost, they stood as a visible symbol to the
utter faithfulness of God, very God. It was the power of His
might and the majesty of His command that held back the
flooding waters of the river while His chosen people crossed
safely on dry ground.

But in a second, significant way the twelve stones were a
stirring reminder of the first steps of unflinching, fearless faith
exercised in God by Israel. They were a silent monument to

this special day on which the people of God boldly placed the soles of their feet in the surging, rushing current of the Jordan, fully confident that God would grant them safe crossing.

Not only would this altar of twelve stones stand as a solid reminder to the present generation of God's total trustworthiness, but also to their posterity throughout all future generations. Their children, grand-children and great grand-children would here recall the mighty miracle performed by God on behalf of their forebears.

The erection of the memorial was not just a ritual. It was a magnificent act of gratitude, praise and acclamation to the goodness and greatness of God. It was stark in its simplicity . . . yet sublime in spiritual significance.

We would do well to emulate Joshua and Israel in this regard. Far too often we quickly forget the great achievements accomplished on our behalf by God. We humans have incredibly short memories when it comes to recalling the blessings of Christ conferred upon us. We so soon let slip from our recollection those special benefits bestowed on us by God's gracious Spirit.

We need to keep some sort of permanent record of the great things our Father has done for us. It is a splendid habit to write them down, to record them in a diary, to keep a permanent reminder of all the wondrous ways in which God has granted us great deliverance. We should not be ashamed to share these stories and retell these events to our families, our friends and even those who know not God, as a witness to the gracious generosity of our loving God!

Such recollections, such accounts, such memorials are not to celebrate our personal piety. They are rendered as a glowing gift of honor to our Father. They are not a means for self-adulation but for the praise of Him who has delivered us. They can be an enormous blessing to God Himself from us His earthly children.

"Bless the LORD, O my soul: and all that is within me, bless His holy name.

Bless the LORD, O my soul, and forget not all His benefits:

Who forgiveth all thine iniquities; who healeth all thy diseases:

Who redeemeth thy life from destruction; who crowneth thee with lovingkindness and tender mercies;

Who satisfieth thy mouth with good things; so that thy youth is renewed like the eagle's" (Psalm 103:1–5).

It is worthy of note here that the erection of the stone memorial at Gilgal was an act in which representatives from all Israel participated. For it was not just Joshua and Caleb and their families who had crossed into Canaan, but all of their fellow tribesmen as well. Though it was Joshua's fearless faith in God which provided such splendid leadership in this memorable event, all of Israel had shared in the triumph which was Jehovah's intention for them. This in and of itself was a beautiful new breakthrough onto new ground for this hapless people.

For his part, Joshua did not gloat over this signal success. It is a measure of the man's magnificent character that he saw the wilderness Exodus as God's great achievement, not his!

To commemorate the occasion as one of special significance for himself, he personally picked up another twelve stones and built a memorial in the very center of the riverbed. It was a solemn gesture of gratitude to God for His vindication of his own quiet confidence in the Almighty.

When the raging floodwaters returned to fill the valley, this humble, hand-built memorial in midstream would soon disappear from sight. As the long years came and went across this burning valley, river silt and mud would settle softly around those stones to entomb them forever.

Yet for Joshua, to the end of his days, and for us, down to this hour, they remain as a sacred spot where a humble yet mighty man gave credit for his conquest of Canaan to his God. For Joshua this was a very private place. It was also a most precious spot. For him it was the pivotal point in his walk with God.

He was not ashamed to establish his own personal witness in this way as to the glory and grandeur of His God. It was a gracious gesture. Nor did it pass unnoticed in the estimation of the Most High.

That day God in turn was to honor and exalt Joshua in the estimation of all his countrymen. No longer was he regarded merely as Moses' protégé. He was seen as more than Moses' first minister. He was recognized now as Israel's supreme commander who moved confidently under the counsel of the Lord Jehovah. For the remaining years of his long and illustrious career he would be held in the highest esteem by Israel as a worthy successor to Moses.

In fact, future events were to demonstrate that this new generation of Israel regarded Joshua with greater respect and reverence than their forefathers ever did Moses. His leadership was never questioned, never challenged. His quiet, strong confidence in God was a steel shaft of loyalty held high for all to see. It challenged every one of his contemporaries to give their total allegiance to Jehovah, and to him.

God always, ever, bestows signal honor upon the individual who seeks no special recognition for himself. His personal commitment to those who serve Him is, "Them that honour me I will honour!" (1 Samuel 2:30).

Part of the great secret of Joshua's startling success under God was his keen sensitivity to the voice of God's Spirit. He was carefully attuned to the commands of the Lord. He was in intimate harmony with His plans and purposes. Whatever clear instructions came to him, he promptly carried out.

In the biblical record left to us from these thrilling times it is noteworthy how often the plain, categorical statement is made: "*The Lord* spake unto Joshua, saying . . . ." We must conclude that such implicit directions came through Eleazer the high priest. Yet they were regarded by Joshua as direct edicts of divine origin. They were never seen as figments of human imagination or the fallible suggestions of human wisdom, much less strange ideas of human invention that were to be questioned.

For Joshua, a forthright man of fearless faith, what God declared, he simply did! It was a brilliant spiritual demonstration of divine "cause" and human "effect." It was the same basic premise to which Christ calls anyone who will know and serve Him: "Ye are my friends, if ye do whatsoever I command you" (John 15:14).

The distinct impression given by this splendid commander is one of a man who, without fanfare or personal flair, delighted in doing as God commanded him. His supreme satisfaction came from loyal service to the Lord. He saw himself as a humble minister of the Most High . . . at the same time a most lofty and noble position among his people.

When, after a long, long day the last of the two million-plus Israelis had crossed the river bed, when the last load of household effects had been carried over, when the last little lamb and stumbling newborn calf of the livestock herds had reached high ground on the other side, Joshua commanded the priests with the ark to come up out of the Jordan.

As their foot soles were lifted up to be set down on the fresh soil of Canaan, the waters of the river rushed into the empty valley floor again. In a thundering roar the dammed-up flood cascaded over the dry crossing ground. All the footprints of the people, all the hoof marks of cattle, sheep, goats and donkeys, even Joshua's monument of twelve river rocks, were quickly covered in a few moments by the swirling, muddy torrent.

Here there could be no turning back to the former wilderness ways. Here there would be no retracing of the tired old desert trails. Here there was no looking back with mournful longing to what they had left behind.

Israel pitched camp that evening for the first time in the new land of promise. Around them were fields of grain ripe and ready for harvest. What a contrast to the thorns and scrub brush of their desert years. Along the river were groves of olives, figs, dates and pomegranates. They were in a region flowing with milk and honey in lavish abundance. It would be a demanding job just to restrain their livestock from stampeding into the lush fields, their children from gorging themselves on fresh fruit and vegetables they had never tasted with their lips and tongues.

For all of Israel this was a celebration unknown before in all their tragic history. It was a day of days to tell and re-tell to all generations!

They had passed from defeat to domination, from tragedy to triumph, from despair to delight—not because they were a great people, but because they had obeyed a great God.

All that He asked now in return was that as His chosen race, they should honor and revere Him. His desire was that this obdurate nation should so love and respect Him that in genuine affection they would "fear" to grieve or offend Him ever. It was He who first loved them. Now all that He asked was that out of gratitude and appreciation they in turn would learn to love and obey Him. Only time would tell.

10

Gilgal

GILGAL WAS THE noble name bestowed on Israel's first beach-head established in enemy territory across the Jordan. Here, on the famous and unforgettable tenth day of the first month of the Hebrew year, Joshua's fighting forces moved onto the land of the Amorites west of the river. It was precisely forty years to the very day that Israel had celebrated the first Passover in Egypt and had gone out in triumph from their grim bondage.

It was God, very God, who had brought them out.

It was God, very God, who now brought them in.

The remarkable aspect of both their Exodus and their entry was that on both occasions the massed multitude moved out and moved in without direct and immediate military attack from the enemy. This highly vulnerable crowd of people, burdened with their household goods, their tiny children, their livestock and their other impedimenta could readily have been massacred in their migration.

But they were not. That is the wonder of it all! And the sole reason for their survival as a nation was the incredible intervention of Jehovah on their behalf. Ever active behind the scenes, moving mightily by His Spirit in the minds and emotions of the Egyptians forty years before, and now among the Amorites and Canaanites, God had granted His people safe passage.

When the flood waters of the Jordan dried up before Israel, so also did the fighting courage, and will to war, of the tribes of Canaan. They were literally paralyzed with terror. So stricken were they with fear and apprehension by the invasion that they never even launched a counterattack against Gilgal.

So, unopposed, in quiet security, the streaming mass of well over two million men, women and children moved relentlessly onto the land west of Jordan. Like an ominous, threatening swarm of voracious desert locusts they struck dread and terror into the enemy.

This formidable feat astonished all the pagan tribes, king-doms and nations of the entire Middle East. From Egypt to Mesopotamia, from Arabia to the Mediterranean coast, word swept across the desert wastes and forested hills that the God of Israel who had delivered His people from Egypt had now brought them into Canaan.

For forty desperate years the pagan world had scoffed and scorned the wretched wanderers in the wilderness. For forty years the hapless Israelis, who had left Egypt with such a high hand only to die in the desert wastes, were a cruel joke to their contemporaries. Especially in Egypt, the reproach and bitter abuse heaped on a people who fled from the fertile Nile delta to merely succumb in the Arabian wastes was relentless. "Where is your God?" was the sinister, cutting charge hurled at them a thousand times.

But that all ended at Gilgal! Now their reproach was rolled away. Now their shame was gone. Israel was on the move in strength under God's mighty outstretched arm. Joshua, within a week, had been empowered to do what Moses failed to achieve in forty, futile years.

It is worthy of note that the society of man always has nothing

but contempt for those who claim to be God's people, yet go
nowhere with Him. The carnal Christian, the half-hearted follower of the Lord, is an object of ridicule to the onlooking
skeptics. Not only are such "half-way people" a pain to themselves but a terrible embarrassment to God.

This new movement of great momentum for Israel was an
opportune moment for them to put their spiritual affairs in
proper order. Joshua was a man sensitive to the Spirit of God.
He was acutely aware that if Israel was to prosper in this new
land of promise, certain significant sacraments of enormous
spiritual import simply had to be given absolute priority. The
first of these was the rite of circumcision. The second was the
passover celebration.

To understand the full impact of the circumcision ceremony
for Israel it is imperative to go back hundreds of years in their
history. It was in God's special call to Abraham, the federal
head of this people, that a covenant had been made to give his
offspring the land of Canaan as an inheritance. This explains
why it was always referred to as "The Land of Promise."

This commitment from Jehovah to Abraham was regarded
always as a solemn, unbreakable covenant on God's part. It was
a token of the special honor bestowed upon Abraham, then
Isaac and Jacob. For this reason Israel always regarded themselves as "God's covenant people—" those of His particular
choice.

As a mark of this special relationship between Abraham and
God, it was ordained from the very outset that each manchild
be circumcised. The rite represented the unique recognition
on man's part that he was no longer a free-will agent to do as he
pleased, but rather "a covenant person" under direction by
divine authority (Genesis 17).

Unhappily for Israel, after leaving Egypt, they constantly
challenged and flagrantly flaunted God's authority and commands. The first most formidable affront to Jehovah was at the

foot of Mount Sinai when they compelled Aaron to fashion a false god for them in the form of a golden bull calf.

Jehovah's immediate response was to disown them. In fact, but for Moses' intervention on Israel's behalf, they would have been wiped out. They were no longer covenant people (Exodus 32–33).

A second equally serious breach of the relationship occurred at Paran. There, after the twelve spies returned, ten of them with a false report of the Promised Land, Israel rebelled against God and demanded a new captain. They insisted they come under new command to one who would lead them directly back into the slime pits of Egypt (Numbers 13–14).

Again God, so insulted and repudiated, was determined to destroy Israel and initiate a new race through Moses. But this humble, meek man reminded Jehovah of His covenant and thus spared the nation a second time.

Nevertheless, because of Israel's unrelenting intransigence and unbelieving disobedience, none of their generation who came out of Egypt, except Joshua and Caleb, were ever to enter Canaan. And a great and significant mark of that dreadful disobedience to the will and purposes of God had been their deliberate refusal to circumcise their children for forty years. They did not see themselves as "covenant people." They did not respect Jehovah as their "covenant God." So they were destined to die in the desert of unbelief and cruel cynicism.

All of this now had to be put right. So during the quiet interlude, after crossing Jordan, while the Canaanites were too terrified to launch a counterattack, all the males in Israel were circumcised. It was a painful operation. It incapacitated the men for days. And, had the Amorites chosen to attack Israel just then, they could readily have slaughtered every man, woman and child in their flimsy desert tents.

Joshua knew full well the enormous risk he took in commanding all of Israel to be circumcised. He was aware of their utter vulnerability. He remembered clearly the ancient account of how Jacob's sons had persuaded the men of Shechem to be circumcised, then annihilated them all when they were still sore and unable to fight back (Genesis 34).

Despite all of this, Joshua was utterly determined to carry out God's commandment in this spiritual rite. He recognized that in crossing Jordan, God's covenant to His people had been consummated. He saw clearly that a new era had been opened before Israel in which they were to be Jehovah's special, "chosen covenant people." He was not ashamed to insist that proudly, gladly they bear the mark which established them in this renewed relationship.

Remarkably, all of Israel consented to go through this rigorous rite. It was a painful ordeal. But it displayed the new and refreshing attitude of compliance with their commander's wishes.

This circumcision ceremony became for Israel a spiritual sacrament of enormous import. In unmistakable terms of profound and painful significance it signaled their identity as God's people. They were intended to be a people set apart to the purposes of God. They were through forever with Egypt or any remote desire to return to its brutal bondage. They were done with the wasted desert days of divided loyalties and divided desires.

In essence, circumcision for Israel in this occasion marked them as dead to the past, and alive, eager to be utterly God's in the future. It was the counterpart to the sacred sacrament of baptism so unique in the spiritual saga of modern day Christians.

It was a titanic turning point upon which the nation's history hinged. Only because of Joshua's fearless faith in God's ability to preserve Israel in this their hour of mortal peril did he proceed with it.

A great part of Joshua's formidable faith had been nourished by the report of his two men who visited Rahab in Jericho. It was they who had come back to give Joshua "God's perspective" of what fear and trepidation gripped the enemy. Through them Joshua had been granted the wide view to see that the Spirit of God had been mightily at work behind the scenes to utterly intimidate the Amorites and Canaanites.

So he now proceeded to celebrate the second great spiritual sacrament for Israel. When the men were whole, Israel would observe the thrilling Passover feast. For this nation it now represented four magnificent demonstrations of Jehovah's utter faithfulness to His followers. 1) The first Passover in Egypt guaranteed that the destroying angel would "pass over" their homes marked with the shed blood of the sacrificial lambs. 2) It marked, too, the night in which they moved out of Egypt and "passed over" the Red Sea to freedom under God. Now the Passover at Gilgal commemorated as well 3) the "passing over" of Jordan to enter the Land of Promise and 4) the "pass over" of an enemy attack that could have annihilated them during circumcision.

In the solemn ceremony of our communion services in the contemporary church, we likewise celebrate the great deliverance granted to us by Christ. He is our Passover Lamb. He is the One who by His death and resurrection brings us from bondage to freedom, from death to life, from despair to delight in a life of joyous new obedience to His will. This is to commemorate His great victory and ours.

As a token and sign of the new life upon which Israel was now embarking, the people gathered up the ripened grain from the fields around Gilgal. With glad abandon they began to feast on the abundance of the fertile soil bequeathed to them by God. Their herds and flocks flourished and fattened in the lush pastures of their new homestead. They went surely and safely into a land flowing with milk and honey. Every promise made to them had been honored by Jehovah.

The very next day no more manna fell upon the ground at dawn. They were done with the old life style. They had embarked on a brand new way of living. It was an exciting and stimulating new adventure.

Joshua had firmly and unflinchingly established the proper priorities for all of Israel. Their spiritual affairs had been given first place. Their proper and appropriate relationship to God has been reestablished. They now stood as an assured people, acutely aware of their allegiance to the Most High. He was their God, their Protector, their Provider.

Now Israel was ready as a nation to move in force against the enemy.

Insofar as Joshua was able he had left no stone unturned to fully prepare Israel for the great battles that lay ahead. By his own unflinching faith and enormous spiritual wisdom, bestowed by God, he had transformed a hapless people into a formidable fighting force.

Before proceeding further with this stirring narrative it is appropriate to pause here briefly to examine the important spiritual truths given to us at Gilgal. Many modern readers are sometimes repulsed by the rite of circumcision. Yet the clear teaching of the New Testament is that it represents genuine repentance. It is a definite turning away from our previous self-centered, willful disobedience to God. It is a deliberate act of self-denial in allowing our wills to be brought into submission to the control of Christ.

This drastic and demanding transaction that takes place within the soul of man has to be a painful, cutting experience. It is more than mere assent to a church creed. It is more than mental understanding of a doctrine. It is really a death to self-assertion . . . a submission to the sovereignty of God's Spirit and the acceptance of God's government in our lives.

The outward evidence we give to our contemporaries of this inner change is the sacrament of baptism. In our soft Western society this rite has little cost attached to it. Amid the fierce pagan peoples of the earth, however, to be baptized is to become a "marked person," often ostracized by society, hated by one's contemporaries and regarded as an enemy.

In profound ways which often escape us entirely, baptism for the believer means total death to the old past life style. It stands for the watershed that divides the empty, wasted desert years from the victorious entry into new territory, moving in strength and triumph under Christ's command.

It is He who makes our victories a reality. It is He who, in going before us, prepares the way to spiritual success. It is He who also, by His might is working within us, causes us to triumph amid all the tests and turmoil of our times.

This is not mere doctrine or theory or theology.

It is the practical application of the power of the risen Christ to our common lives. He who died and rose again is alive and at work in our experience to great victory. We celebrate this continually in joy and gratitude with our communion ceremonies. Bless His Name! (Colossians 2:9–15).

11

Jericho Falls

ACROSS THE LOW plain, a short distance from Gilgal, stood Jericho. Its perimeter of rough brown walls, pierced by huge gateways, now barred and bolted, looked impregnable. Like a tawny, maned lion, crouched upon the hot valley floor, it was a formidable fortress.

At sunset, when the long evening shadows stretched out darkly beyond its rugged ramparts, Jericho looked even more resolute. Joshua had no battering rams to assault the city. He possessed no engines of war to scale the walls. His warriors knew nothing of long sieges in battle.

Alone with his thoughts, Israel's new commander walked out into the dusk to meditate over his next move against the enemy citadel. It was one thing to cross a river unopposed. It was quite another to storm a walled, fortress city full of armed warriors.

As is common with men in deep thought, Joshua walked slowly, his eyes cast down upon the ground. His sandaled feet kicked up small puffs of dust from the hot soil. What should his strategy be? He needed wisdom and skill far beyond his own devising.

Suddenly his reverie was cut short. Lifting his gaze from the ground momentarily, he found himself face to face with a warrior fully armed. His sword was drawn ready to strike. In an immediate flash of swift subconscious reaction Joshua, too, drew his sword and challenged the stranger.

"Are you for or against us?" he growled, ready to leap to the attack like a leopard.

The armed man replied boldly: "I Am; The Captain of the Lord's Host, has come to your side."

In shock, amazement and awe Joshua flung himself face down before the celestial commander. He was in the presence of heaven's potentate. In total obeisence he prostrated himself before his Lord.

"What are your orders, Lord?" Joshua asked in wonderment. He was ready to respond at once to any command that came from his High Command.

"Remove your sandals, stained and soiled. You are on sacred ground in this spot!"

Promptly Joshua complied. As he slipped his feet from the footgear that had not worn out in forty years of tough desert travel, another stirring scene flashed across the memory of his mind. He recalled the awesome day, often retold by Moses, when he had stood, alarmed, before the burning bush. There came to Moses then the same identical command Joshua now received, "I Am—*the* Lord Jehovah—I Am here."

Joshua was in the presence of God, very God. He was standing now at attention before the supreme commander of all the unseen spiritual forces of the universe. He was being alerted to the angelic host available to him in this crucial hour under the captaincy of Jehovah.

Momentarily the Lord God of heaven, in human disguise, revealed to Israel's new commander that the formidable forces of the supernatural world stood beside him. As with Elisha many years later, a vision was granted to his servant to see the

chariots and horsemen of the armies of God which surrounded
them in safety.

Joshua never forgot this encounter. He was not fighting
alone. In every engagement he could count on supernatural
forces acting as his allies. It was an insight that gave Joshua
incredible courage and confidence in all his future conquests.

This acute awareness of Christ, "The Captain of our Salvation," ever with us in the conflicts of life is a reality few of God's
people relish or rely on. Yet it is the supreme secret to success
and triumph in our troubled world. His own word to us is, "Lo,
I am with you alway, even unto the end of the world." (Matthew
28:20). Again He has declared, "I will not leave you comfort-
less: I will come to you" (John 14:18).

Immediately Jehovah made clear to Joshua exactly how
Jericho should be taken. To anyone else the strategy might
have seemed absurd and laughable. But not to this stalwart of
such resolute faith in God.

First and foremost the divine declaration made to him was
that not only would the city fall before him, but so also would
its king and all his armed men of valor. It would be a total
triumph. But it would take unusual tactics and an extended
time span to achieve victory.

The plan was laid out precisely for Joshua and his people.
Their part was to comply with the clear-cut commands from on
high. They were not normal battle plans, but they would prevail. Simple, implicit cooperation on Israel's side was essential
to success.

Most significant was that the action would not all be over in a
day. For, though Jericho was a formidable fortified city, it only
covered about 320 acres of land. Its turreted walls could be
encircled quite readily in about an hour's march, even allowing
for the slower pace of the women and children who brought up
the rear guard group in going around the city.

The exact order in which Israel would march was of interest.

The advance troops were Israel's armed men, roughly half a million foot soldiers. Then came seven white-robed priests blowing eerie battle calls on rough ram horns. Behind them the sacred ark of God, the remarkable emblem of the presence of the Most High, was borne aloft by the priests. Gathered on the fringes were the massed multitudes of Israel's aged men, women and children. All were to have their taste of victory.

The massed multitude was to march in silence for six days. Only the weird, wild notes from the crude rams' horn trumpets rose above the ominous, muffled *"TRAMP—TRAMP—TRAMP"* of four million feet pounding the ground into powdery dust.

It might have been much more pleasant for the people to relax in the shade of their tents. After all, there was ripe grain to grind, fresh bread to bake, delicious fruit to enjoy and herds to milk. Why not just let Jericho, gripped with fear and panic, perish by slow starvation within its own walls? Why bother battering the buttresses to the ground? Why march around this citadel in the dust and heat while the enemy scoffed and hurled insults at them from the top of the walls?

Such questions never surfaced here. These were the kind of complaints that this whimsical people might have hurled at Moses in his melancholy moments. But they dared not challenge Joshua, their new and fearless commander, with such criticism. What he said, they did. And this was because he was a man under God's authority. Whatever Jehovah decreed, Joshua did. The divine chain of command functioned with utter fidelity.

For six consecutive, hot, blistering days Israel circled Jericho. It demanded discipline. It called for consistency. It took time and trouble and endurance, all without any apparent results. Nothing seemed to happen.

But on the seventh day the total strategy changed. Instead of marching around the wretched, sunbaked walls that radiated waves of reflected heat, only once, for about an hour, the exercise would consume most of the day. It would be a tedious, tiresome tramp that circled the city seven times for at least seven or eight solid hours. It would be a day-long ordeal of well over twenty miles march. Israel would be tired, dusty, thirsty and on the point of exhaustion.

As they circled the walls for a seventh time on the seventh day the people were commanded to shout the cry of victory. The thunderous roar that rose in a surging crescendo from two million parched throats, choked with dust, was a harsh and discordant cacophony of sound. It obliterated and drowned out the trumpet blasts. But it was the vocal, audible declaration of conquest!

In an earth-shaking rumble the great high walls of Jericho began to crack, then crumble. It was as if they had been rocked with a gigantic seismic wave. The turrets began to lean inward then tumbled into thunderous clouds of brick, mortar and dust.

En masse the Israelis turned and drew their swords. Amid the rising clouds of dust, each armed man slashed and fought his way into the heart of the city. No one was to be spared . . . only the harlot Rahab and her family, safely ensconced in her humble home on the city wall.

By an act of providential intervention, the only part of the walled fortress which did not crash to the ground was where the prostitute lived. Her small section of the crude wall still stood amid all the ruins around it. From the window there still dangled the scarlet rope upon which the two spies escaped to safety. Now coated in dust, it still remained in place, the emblem of security upon which Rahab's own escape from disaster depended.

The two bold young spies and their comrades rushed into the ruins, raced up the cracked steps to her house, and brought out Rahab and all her family. Amid the mayhem and slaughter they alone were spared. The promise of security given by the spies was fully vindicated.

No doubt a thousand times, during those seven dreadful days of siege, Rahab had looked down on the marching mob below and wondered how she would be rescued. A thousand times her heart must have trembled at the "tramp—tramp—tramp" of the pounding feet outside her walls. A thousand times she must have fingered the red rope tied in her window, making sure it was still there, reassuring her fluttering heart that her help would come from the Lord God of Israel in whom her confidence reposed.

Her faith was vindicated as she stood safely with her family outside the flattened city walls. She had been brought from death to life, from despair to love, from degradation to exaltation.

She, who had been a harlot in Jericho, would be an honored mother in Israel.

For Joshua and for all of Israel, the destruction of Jericho was a classic confirmation, too, of their confidence in God. The armies of Israel had not resorted to the strategy of man or the ingenuity of military inventions to achieve victory. Rather, their triumph came through calm and implicit compliance with the commands of God.

It was a stunning and brilliant demonstration of what simple cooperation and outright obedience to God can accomplish in impossible situations. This explains why the startling New Testament record of this remarkable victory sums it all up in one short statement: "By faith the walls of Jericho fell down, after they were compassed about seven days" (Hebrews 11:30).

Two aspects of this episode which are worthy of special note are:

1) the quiet perseverance which ultimately prevailed. Jericho did not fall in a day, nor two or three. In fact it was encircled thirteen times before victory came. This alone

should dissuade anyone from believing that "13" is an unfortunate figure. But it does also show that we must not always expect "instant results" in our walk of faith with God.

His repeated promise to Israel had been that He would drive out the enemy little by little, one step at a time. We would do well to remind ourselves of this often. Most of us expect far too much too soon. Let us learn to live quietly in happy harmony with the pace of progress our Father sets for us.

2) The second remarkable lesson is that when in fact we do capitulate to the Captain of our souls, when we do allow Christ to actually control our lives, He brings to our aid enormous resources far beyond our own ability.

In reality it was God's wisdom, God's Spirit, God's power, God's presence, God's hand at work behind the walls of Jericho that finally flattened them. It was in truth, and in actual fact, God who gave Israel this tremendous triumph.

The one explicit command given to Israel which may well have been the most difficult to carry out had to do with the prizes of conquest. Joshua instructed his people very carefully that all the spoils of war from this initial engagement belonged not to them, but to God.

This, in essence, was simply a restatement in concrete terms of the truth that the honor, the credit, the reward of victory belongs not to man but to God. It was He alone who was worthy of this honor. Jehovah deserved to have the gold and silver, brass and iron vessels dedicated to His service. And anyone daring to covetously plunder such booty for himself was in fact depriving God of His just dues.

It was not that the Almighty was impoverished and in need of gold and silver won in war. Rather, the concept was that, as a mark of esteem and respect for His might, the best man could do was devote all the precious metals to the Most High. This Joshua decreed should be done.

It was a humble layman's way of declaring unequivocally

that the battle for Jericho was essentially God's conquest. The Lord of Hosts, the Captain of the armies of God, the Man with the drawn sword had achieved for Israel what Israel could never have achieved alone and on her own. Therefore He and He alone deserved to be honored and acclaimed with all the prizes of war.

This was a daring stand for Joshua to make. It was to fly in the face of all convention and tradition. Every native impulse in the inflamed hearts of the victorious Israelis would prompt them to plunder and loot for their own selfish ends.

But even more than this was Joshua's solemn declaration that this city of the Jordan plain should never, ever be raised from its ruins again by the hand of man. Anyone who tried would be cursed.

What God had chosen to demolish no man should restore.

The net result of Jericho's fall was that Joshua's fame as a brilliant leader, who enjoyed God's comradeship, swept across the whole country. Joshua was not just an ordinary general on his own mission. He was a formidable commander, bold under God.

12

Achan

FROM ALL OUTWARD appearances, it would seem at this stage of Israel's horrendous history that this nation was now at the pinnacle of power. It was as though no force could stand before them. No obstacle could prevent them from achieving any objective they desired. In a word, they seemed invincible.

Yet it was not to be!

For within her ranks' was a man, Achan by name, who willfully, secretly and covetously had claimed some booty from the ruins of Jericho for himself.

The sight of a gorgeous scarlet cloak from Babylon, the glitter of a golden ingot, the sparkle of silver coins had attracted his attention, aroused his avarice. Surely no great harm could come from laying hold of this loot for his own use.

After all, was he not a man of war? Had he not risked his life in crossing Jordan? Was he not entitled to the spoils of war now that the city of Jericho had fallen? Didn't tradition dictate that booty was the reward of battle? Why should he necessarily capitulate to Joshua's commands about common people avoiding the accursed belongings of the Amorites?

These and a score of other reasons raced through Achan's mind and rationale. He was a thoroughly pragmatic person who felt sure Joshua's ban on any man seizing the spoils of battle from the ruined city was unwarranted.

So while his comrades in arms gathered up whatever gold, silver, bronze or iron implements they could find, to be dedicated to Jehovah with joy, Achan was furtively sneaking off with some loot to his tent. Amid all the chaos and confusion of the conquest this may not have been too difficult to do. Men were rushing hither and thither. The mobs of Israel were scrambling over the mounds of rubble that remained in heaps where a city once stood. The dead and dying were lying in agony under the scorching sun.

Swiftly, surely, with a few stabbing strokes of his sword, Achan dug a hole in the new soil of the Promised Land that lay within his tent. Not only could this precious fresh earth produce milk and honey in bountiful abundance to feed his family, it could also conceal his guilt and cover his bold-faced crime against his God. Or so he thought!

Without a doubt Achan was watched by his family as he hid the forbidden wealth within their home. Sternly he swore his wife and his sons and daughters to total secrecy. Their utter silence would be a sure guarantee of their future wealth. For even at today's deflated values, the booty he buried would be worth roughly $25,000.00.

The gorgeous gown at least		$500.00.
The silver coins about		$3,500.00.
The wedge of gold		$21,000.00.
	Total	25,000.00

Finally, in an act of misguided presumption and outright defiance, Achan had carefully covered the spoil with the soft, mellow earth, then walked on it to pack it flat. Again his malicious mind, blinded by the sudden wealth, distorted by his own self-deception, convinced him that he could lay claim to this forbidden contraband.

104

"Didn't God say that any place I set down the sole of my foot He would give to me?" Persistently he paced back and forth over the freshly packed earth beneath his sandals. Didn't God say that I would gain anything I was bold enough to step out and tread upon? Surely it must be perfectly legitimate for me to lay claim to that which I now have buried beneath my feet.

Completely convinced that his deliberate disobedience was morally justified, Achan smiled softly to himself. His future was totally assured. This was a secret store of wealth that would stand him in good stead.

Little did he know it would soon see him dead!

Jericho stood out stark and grim on the burning plain. It was no longer a great high-walled city. Instead it was but a mass of ruined rubble. Crows and vultures wheeled on dark wings over the ghastly ruins. Here and there they settled on a carcass of man or beast to gorge and quarrel over the offal. By night jackals yapped in glee as they gorged on the grisly remains. Hyenas howled amid the ruined walls and piles of rubble.

It was not the sort of spot Joshua and his people cared to stop.

It had been stripped and reduced to an utter waste.

Beyond it lay the town of Ai, a much smaller community that could no doubt be captured with comparative ease.

As was his custom, Joshua sent off several of his warriors to reconnoiter the little city. They did not even bother to try and penetrate the town. Instead, in a rather casual, cursory way, they simply viewed it from a distance. It seemed so small, so defenseless, so vulnerable that it could be taken in a single lightning attack with a small handful of men.

At most the spies suggested that a minimal force of about three thousand armed men should be sent ahead to sack Ai. It would be all over in a matter of hours. After all, the enemy were but a tiny band of frightened men.

Joshua, apparently totally unaware of Achan's action, perhaps a bit flushed and overconfident with the conquest of Jericho, and no doubt zealous and keen to maintain his momentum in the conquest of Canaan, sent off three thousand men in a precipitous attack against Ai.

It was a hasty decision. Apparently it was not based on seeking the guidance of God. And the report given to him was distorted because of the willful intransigence of Achan's family whose flagrant affront to God now jeopardized all of Joshua's leadership.

When the Israelis attacked Ai they were thrown back in their tracks. They were met with a ferocious counterattack by the men in Ai. Taken off guard, Joshua's warriors turned their backs and fled for their lives. Thirty-six of them lay dead upon the ground.

It all happened so quickly Joshua was totally undone. In a matter of hours his fighting forces had turned from being triumphant victors to craven cowards.

Where before the heart and will of the Canaanites had been gripped with fear and panic, now suddenly the tables were turned. Israel was paralyzed with apprehension. Their will to war had turned to water, leaving them a hapless prey to wild fears and foreboding speculation.

Most astonishing was Joshua's personal reaction to this defeat. In dismay he flung himself down into the dust. He tore his tunic in despair. Then tossing handfuls of dust into his hair he lay prostrate before the ark of God until sundown.

These were the actions of a man deep in mourning. Death had come to Israel. Death had come to all his own dreams of conquest. Death had come to the leadership entrusted to him by Jehovah. Death had come to Israel's reputation as a fearless conquering force.

In reproach and remorse, Joshua, in a moment of rash weakness, accused God, very God, of bringing Israel to such an impasse. Despite all his previous loyalty and utter devotion to the Most High, Joshua suddenly in a fit of despair, charged Jehovah with the disaster. It was an ignominious reflection on this commander who had otherwise showed such formidable faith. It simply was not in keeping with his sterling character!

Momentarily Joshua even questioned the integrity of God in bringing Israel over the Jordan. Surely it was not His intention that His people become an easy prey to the Canaanites? It might have been better never to have left the wilderness! And most important, what of God's own great name and honor? Was it to be discredited and maligned by the gloating Amorites?

This harangue was totally out of character for Joshua.

Nor was God about to enter any prolonged dialogue with Joshua about it.

Instead the divine edict which came was cutting, fierce and direct.

"Get up off your face. Israel has sinned. Get rid of the wrong in your midst. You will know only defeat until this is done."

No doubt this divine disclosure of the cause for Israel's debacle came as a shocking surprise to Joshua. Up to this point he had enjoyed implicit and wholehearted cooperation from his contemporaries in whatever he commanded them. This act of Achan's was the first breach of command both to him and to the Lord.

The remedy required to right the wrong was severe. First the entire company of people would have to be cleansed and sanctified in a spiritual ritual. Then by the drawing of lots under Eleazer, it would be decided who the offender was in Israel. He must pay the supreme death penalty for the loss of thirty-six lives endured by the nation in its attack on Ai.

Joshua was up long before dawn on this ominous day. No longer did he lie flat on his face in fear. This would be a dreadful ordeal. Choosing out, then condemning a man and his family to oblivion was an onerous order for any commander. But Joshua was determined justice should be done. The one responsible for betraying the strength and security of his brothers in battle would pay with his own blood. It was the straightforward out-working of the irrevocable laws of divine retribution.

Lot by lot the choice was narrowed down. First the tribe of Judah was chosen; then the family of the Zarhites; then the clan leader Zabdi; and finally the Lord's lot, drawn under the divine guidance of Urim, fell on Achan. It was a formidable process of unerring accuracy.

Firmly Joshua commanded the stricken man not only to make full confession of the crime committed but also to bring out the booty hidden in his tent as evidence for all to see his wrong-doing. In this way all of Israel would participate in the full execution of justice.

It was imperative for Israel to understand the ominous gravity of Achan's deliberate disobedience. His self-indulgence had brought fear and defeat to all his comrades. It had cost thirty-six of them their very lives. Now he, his family and all his possessions would be forfeited. He who had wrought such havoc in Israel would pay the penalty by annihilation and total obliteration.

To narrate this event in a simple historical record is one thing. To draw from the account certain profound spiritual principles is another. Such sad scenes have been imbedded in the story of God's dealing with Israel, in order that others at a later date might learn spiritual truth from them.

It is appropriate at this point for us to grasp clearly what God's Spirit reveals to us in the tragedy of Achan (his name means "trouble" or "the troubler").

First and foremost is the profound principle that no person is a private island of independent action limited to his or her own interests. Whatever we do touches other lives, either for good or for evil. How we spend our time and strength counts for Christ or counts against Him. There is no neutral ground!

Modern man's suggestion that we are free to live as we like is a diabolical deception that spells out unspeakable suffering for those who flagrantly indulge in self-gratification. It brings awesome agony to others all around them.

Second, this event in the history of Israel demonstrates very vividly the horrendous consequences of deliberate disobedience to the will and purposes of God. The ultimate consequences of wrong-doing are shattering. As I have stated again and again in my books, man does not break the laws and edicts of God with impunity. It is they which ultimately not only break the offender, but consign him to oblivion, blown away in the fierce and irrevocable outworking of eternal justice.

It is a straightforward case of cause and effect.

"The soul that sinneth, it shall die" (Ezekiel 18:4).

Present day pastors, teachers and evangelists fail to impress on their listeners the terrible consequences of wrongdoing. They speak softly of sin as though it were nothing more than mere human weakness, winked at, and easily overlooked by a loving, compassionate Christ.

Not so! Divine justice demands full retribution for wrong done. And the cost for such justice to be carried out is death. Either ours or another's. For the one prepared to voluntarily confess and make restitution there comes clemency.

This is because of the appalling price paid for us by God in Christ at Calvary. But without confession of wrong, without genuine repentance of conduct, without deep remorse of spirit, culminating in conversion of conduct, none of God's mercy avails. Simply because it has not been accepted or claimed in an act of faith by the offender.

Achan refused to come clean except under coercion. He had no great pangs of conscience. His misdeed was a deliberate act of his will. In response to his own determination for self-gratification he brought enormous evil on all his associates. He also brought shameful reproach to God. Yet he never seemed grieved by his own greed.

Third, it is most instructive for us to realize that even a man of Joshua's caliber has feet of clay. Despite his unflinching faith in God up to this time, despite his remarkable loyalty to Jehovah, despite his own incredible courage in the past, he here fell flat on his face in despair.

Even though Joshua and Israel had entered Canaan in triumph, tasted of its fragrant fields and orchards, known great victory over Jericho, they could still fall flat before their adversaries. This comes to us as a solemn, serious warning from God's Spirit. In 1 Corinthians 10:11–12 we are told clearly: "Now all these things happened unto them for ensamples: and they are written for our admonition, upon whom the ends of the world are come. Wherefore let him that thinketh he standeth take heed lest he fall."

It is incumbent upon us as God's children to walk humbly with Christ. We need always to seek the direction of His Spirit in our decisions. Always we must keep our Father's perspective and view of life.

This brings us to the fourth principle worthy of note here. In haste and without due consultation with Eleazer, Joshua had sent off the spies to Ai. Acting on their wrong advice, basing his strategy on their deceptive view, his forces suffered casualties.

It is easy for any of us to become overconfident. It is often a temptation for us to take matters into our own hands and make hasty, ill-conceived decisions. Often these are beclouded by arrogance or self-assertion. The consequences can be calamitous.

We have to learn, often through trial and error, that if we are to succeed with God in the conflicts of life, we must keep pace with Him. It is He who must make clear to us always what our course of action should be. This God did in due course for Joshua at Ai, but the initial setback had been severe and shattering.

13

Ai Is Ambushed

THE EPISODE with Achan made an indelible mark on Joshua. He was far too wise a leader ever to forget the lesson learned with such stern severity. From now on, even more than ever before, he would carefully seek the clear and unmistakable guidance of God in every move he made.

It came as a remarkable consolation to Joshua that though he and Israel had fallen before the foe, though they had failed to comply implicitly with Jehovah's commands, though there had been tragedy rather than triumph in the initial assault on Ai, they were not utterly forsaken of God.

Again, as so often before, the grand and generous words of encouragement came to the contrite commander: *"Fear not, neither be thou dismayed: take all your men of war and go up against Ai. See I have given you its king, the city, all its people, and their land."*

It was the stirring, exciting, stimulating encouragement which he so desperately needed in the hour of dark despair after their ignominious defeat.

Precisely the same can be true for us. There will be times when we fall prey to temptation; when we are overwhelmed because of our own waywardness; when we fail to fulfill our Father's finest intentions for us. These are tragic times both for Him and us. Yet they need not be terminal in impeding our forward progress.

In our spiritual walk with God, Christ comes to us by His Spirit, upon our confession of wrongdoing and repentance (quitting) of evil, to assure us of forgiveness. His word to us is to arise, stand on our feet, and begin again to take territory with Him.

The opportunity for progress remains open to us.

But the fact remains that the recovery of lost ground is always painful and costly. Still we put our hand in God's hand and press on.

A parallel which helps us to understand this principle is that of a loving parent with a young and willful child. Even though the youngster falls flat in the dust, he is not left there to cry and struggle alone. Rather the compassionate parent rushes over to pick him up, hugs him with reassurance, wipes away the tears, brushes off the clinging dirt, and sets him on his feet again, encouraging him to walk bravely once more.

It is true there may very well be a swift stroke of discipline, a stern word of rebuke, a severe look of reproach. But once the correction of wrong is over there comes only encouragement to carry on. And so it is also with us and our Father God.

He takes no delight in our disasters.

He finds no pleasure in our distress.

He longs only to pick us up and set us on our way again in joyous company with Himself.

This was likewise true for Joshua and all of Israel.

Explicit and meticulous instructions were given as to the exact strategy and tactics to be used in the capture of Ai. These divine directions may have seemed a bit absurd, and for Joshua extremely humiliating. But he was not about to debate the issue with God. He himself was a man under command.

Though Ai had only about twelve-thousand armed men to guard her defenses, Joshua was clearly instructed to take all of Israel's six-hundred thousand men into action. Thus the overwhelming odds against the enemy were about fifty to one. It was a bit like the old adage of using a sledgehammer to swat a single fly.

This in itself was a most embarrassing action. Even with a simple "walk-over" victory it was not the sort of triumph to enhance anyone's record.

Second, the strategy to be used was one of deceit and subversion. Instead of an outright frontal assault, Ai was to be taken by ambush. It was a military maneuver that would be carried out under cover of darkness.

None of these tactics were the sort normally employed by forces with enormous military superiority. They were, instead, the cunning and craftiness used when a force was heavily outnumbered.

Joshua knew all about this. And it is a mark of the man's genuine humility before God that he did not hesitate to comply promptly with such subversive strategy. The road to recovery of his honor and prestige was one of painful self-abnegation.

Happily for this stalwart of such fearless faith, he was totally convinced that the divine key to his spiritual and military success was simply to do God's bidding. In the eyes of the enemy, and in the estimation of his own followers, he might appear as a fool. But above all else Joshua was prepared to implicitly carry out God's commands no matter the cost of personal condescension.

It was the formula for fantastic results.

Not only would there be victory in the place of defeat, but also there would be the additional reward of taking the spoils of war from Ai. This was in some measure a happy compensation for his humiliation.

Where before Israel had been strictly forbidden to loot or

pillage Jericho, here that edict was removed and the invaders would be given a free hand to plunder the captured city and claim their prize of battle.

Perhaps the crestfallen people needed this new incentive as an encouragement to go against the enemy again. The exciting prospect of taking crops and livestock, gold and silver, clothing and furniture for themselves was a strong and heady stimulant for combat.

With all of this in mind, Joshua dispatched a contingent of thirty thousand men to ambush Ai. They were instructed to take cover in the rough terrain lying to the west of Ai and Bethel, another small town near Ai. Their clear instructions were to lay low until the main contingent of Joshua's forces fled from before Ai and thus drew the defenders from the city in hot pursuit.

Then, at a prearranged signal from Joshua, who would raise aloft his battle javelin in a gesture of triumph, they were to rise up from hiding and sack the unguarded, open city. Meanwhile, Joshua and his forces, seeing Ai on fire would turn to attack the enemy, now trapped between the two Israeli contingents behind and before Ai.

It was a tense time for Joshua. He was not inclined to remain aloof from those under his new command. Like himself they had been shaken by the death of their comrades who attacked Ai the first time. So to supply moral support Joshua took a careful census of his men, then led them into position north of Ai. They camped on a rise of ground across from Ai.

As with Jericho, so here, Joshua went out alone into the valley that lay between his forces and the enemy. Here he communed quietly with God, beseeching Him to grant a great victory the next day. In fact, what he was doing was to set his feet upon the ground around Ai, claiming it in faith for Israel.

At dawn the next day, the warriors of Ai streamed out of their fortress gates to attack Joshua's forces who were in full view across the valley. Precisely as planned, the Israelis fled in mock panic and disarray. The men of Ai were sure there would be another massacre so they cast discretion to the winds. Leaving their town open and totally vulnerable to attack, they pursued Joshua.

Suddenly the embattled commander halted in mid-flight. In a bold gesture of defiance he flung up his right arm clutching his shining war spear. Glinting in the morning sun, it was the signal for the men in ambush to storm the city. They rushed from hiding, poured through the open gates, set the town on fire with torches and hastily looted everything of value.

In consternation the men of Ai looked over their shoulders to see dark columns of ominous smoke rising above their city walls. In an instant they realized their dilemma. For now Joshua's main army had turned in flight to slaughter them in deadly hand-to-hand combat. Demoralized with fear, rushing here and there in blind panic, the entire force of twelve thousand men were annihilated by sundown.

Joshua, charged with the heady wine of victory, held his battle arm aloft, his spear outstretched, as a sign of total conquest. As his men charged and fought the foe he urged them on in triumph. It was an exact replay of his own first stirring triumph at Rephidim when Moses, his commander, held his arms aloft in a symbol of victory under Jehovah.

Once more God had shown Himself strong, mighty to prevail on behalf of His chosen people. Once more Joshua's fearless faith in the Most High had been vindicated. Once more, now for the third time, new territory had been taken, productive ground had been gained and the reward was a bounty of booty to be distributed among all the Israelis.

As a final gesture of total triumph, the captured king of Ai was hanged on a tree in full view for all to see. Then at sunset, in strict accord with the Mosaic laws, his body was removed.

Thrown down in shame at the main gate of the smoldering, ruined city, the corpse was covered with a huge mound of loose rock and rubble.

Like the pile of stones at the Jordan crossing it would stand as a solemn memorial to all future generations, that, in this place God wrought an overwhelming victory for His people who obeyed Him.

This was the first, formidable victory in actual armed combat for Israel in Canaan. The fall of Jericho had, in essence, been a spectacular, supernatural miracle performed by the almighty hand of God. Israel had here learned the basic spiritual lesson—that to overcome one has to obey God. There are no other options open to us. God's people may try all sorts of other tactics, but only compliance with His commands assures us of conquest.

To bring this cardinal concept home clearly to all the people under his command, Joshua did not celebrate with a victory march or dazzling banquet. Instead he did a most unusual thing.

He built a simple, crude, rugged altar of twelve uncut, unchiselled stones. No tool ever touched the rough rocks in an attempt to fit them together. They were raw field stones dug from the fertile soil of the new land God had given Israel in keeping with His covenant to them, and their federal forebear Abraham.

For it was in this spot, in the vale of Shechem, lying between the twin hills of Mt. Gerizim and Mt. Ebal, that Abraham had camped nearly eight hundred years before. Here, between Ai and Bethel, God had promised His friend, the great patriarch, that this rich land would become the inheritance of his offspring (see Genesis 12:6–9).

In strict compliance with the instructions of Moses, Joshua now offered sacrifices of burnt offerings and peace offerings to

Jehovah. At last, at long last, after hundreds of years of agony and anguish Israel had come home to her rightful inheritance and proper resting place.

This was no isolated commemoration of a single triumph over Ai. It was, rather, a magnificent ceremony marking the final culmination of eight hundred years of horrendous history for a perverse and petulant people. Only the unfailing perseverance of a long-suffering God could have accomplished this long and sad ordeal.

The vale of Shechem, lying tranquil and serene between the two sheltering mounts on either side, has been considered by many to be the most beautiful location in all of Palestine. It forms a natural amphitheatre, in which a massed multitude of people could clearly be addressed without assistance from any man-made-sound amplifiers.

Here Joshua arranged for all of Israel, as well as the foreigners who had recently joined their ranks, to be assembled. In a solemn and serious ceremony Joshua again prepared two tablets of stone upon which were inscribed again the mighty Ten Commandments of the Most High. Just as these ordinances of God had been the basic standard of behavior for Israel during the forty years of their wilderness wanderings, so now the same essential code of conduct applied in this their Land of Promise. Nothing had changed, they were put out in plain view for all to see. What applied to Israel applied equally to the strangers now living among them. (To use New Testament terminology, God's directions were as valid for the Gentile as for the Jew.)

Joshua consummated the celebration ceremony, not with singing and dancing, not with laughter and hilarity, not with flag-waving and wine-drinking, but with a most moving recitation of all the ordinances of God given to them through Moses.

In clear, distinct, trumpetlike syllables that every man, woman and child could understand, all the laws and commandments of the Lord were read in their hearing. Not one soul among all the multitude could ever say they were not familiar with the Word of God.

This divine declaration of God's purposes for His people was ever to be the source of their strength, the wisdom of their lives, the ultimate criteria of all their conduct.

In this celebration Joshua declared unequivocally to all his followers exactly what God Himself had declared to him:

> *"Observe to do all that is written in this word—*
> *then you will make your way prosperous—*
> *then you will enjoy great success."*

14

The Gibeonites
Deceive Joshua

ANYONE WHO HAS read the biblical account of Israel's occupation of Canaan under Joshua's command may experience a degree of revulsion at the apparent ruthlessness of the invasion. It may well seem that the virtual annihilation of entire communities was overly drastic and unbecoming to those who were God's chosen people.

To understand, even partially, what was taking place it is imperative to pause here briefly in an attempt to explain the ferocious conquest of Canaan. It may help the reader to see things from God's perspective.

First, there is the bedrock violence of human nature. In his unregenerate condition, man is a fierce predator. Human societies have always invaded, plundered and pillaged their neighbors, the stronger overpowering the weaker. The entire community of men upon the earth have had a horrendous history of one race overrunning another in wave upon wave of annihilation.

Witness the occupation of the North American continent by the settlers from Europe. Read the blood-red story of the subjugation of the red men, the cruel and heartless extermination of entire tribes of noble, dignified, primitive Indian tribes. Today hardly a single survivor remains of the Chumash Indians who once occupied the lovely, sun-kissed shores of Southern California.

It is all a part of the pattern of death, violence and cruelty inherent in human conduct. God our Father looks upon our human mayhem with unutterable anguish. He who sees when even a sparrow falls from its nest, grieves over the unbridled vindictiveness of human nature (Genesis 6:5–6 and Romans 3:9–19).

Second, amid the specter of endless death and destruction, for reasons known only to Him, God chooses to use one nation or race or people to chasten and judge another. More often than not, He appears to prefer this rather than inflicting direct disaster on those who do evil deliberately.

Of course there are exceptions to the rule: the catastrophic flood in Noah's time; the destruction of Sodom and Gomorrah with fire and brimstone; the slaughter of all Egypt's firstborn by the destroying angel are cases where the apocalyptic judgment of the Most High was executed apart from the act of man.

But the fact remains that God permits and arranges for one community to scourge, chastise and even annihilate another, in order to execute judgment. Just as Israel became a terror to the Amorites and Canaanites so in turn they would be invaded and well-nigh exterminated by the pagan powers of Assyria and Babylon (See Isaiah 10:5–7).

Third, it is essential to see that such drastic measures are meted out in response to the rebellion which openly defies the edicts of God's divine purposes. It is not that He is unmerciful or vindictive. Rather, quite the opposite, He is persevering, longsuffering and gracious in dealing with even the most obtuse people.

In Noah's day his contemporaries were given years and years of opportunity to repent. But they would not! Sodom and

Gomorrah would have been spared had even ten residents responded to the pleas of righteous Lot. Egypt and Pharaoh were given nine warning plagues before the tenth terrible holocaust.

Likewise for the Canaanites and Amorites. They knew full well of all the fierce judgments that came through the flood, the fire, the annihilation of Egypt's firstborn. But they had not been moved to seek Jehovah God. They, like Israel, had seen and heard and knew the testimony of Abraham, Isaac and Jacob. Yet they turned not to serve the Lord. These pagan races in willful perversion had turned instead to false gods, to bestial human sacrifices, to sexual aberrations of all sorts, to gross evil of the worst kind.

The cup of their iniquity had overflowed. So now in response the cup of divine judgment was to be poured out upon them. God's direct instructions to Joshua were simply to liquidate the offenders.

The only survivors would be those rare remnants like Rahab and her family, who turned in faith to trust their lives to the Lord God of Israel. They, in the midst of death found life; from pagan perversion they stepped into a new way of life with God's people; from despair and degradation they came into dignity and decency, under the laws of God.

Always, ever, God makes it possible for a remnant to survive. He calls to all men; He entreats all people; His Spirit appeals in sundry ways to all sorts. Only a few respond. His narrow way is chosen only by a handful, though He flings wide His arms to welcome any who may care to come to Him.

Among the Canaanites, there was one small group who knew full well the inevitable destruction that lay ahead for them. The people of Gibeon were sure that they would be wiped out by Joshua's forces just as Jericho and Ai had been. The Israeli invaders would not spare a man, woman or child among them. So in craftiness and cunning they turned to subterfuge to survive.

It was not to serve God that they turned to trickery, but simply to save their own skins. It was not to follow the precepts of the living God that they decided to approach Joshua and sue for peace, but simply to escape obliteration. There was method in their apparent madness. That was to outwit the invaders.

Picking a handful of weather-worn men, they dressed them in tattered clothing, threadbare with age and wear. On their feet they slipped shoddy old sandals ragged with long treks across rocky terrain . . . battered and wrecked by a thousand boulders.

Selecting the most wretched and aged asses they could find, they flung old tattered sacks across their blistered backs. These they loaded with ancient saddle pouches that bore stale, dry and moldy bread. The little wobbly kneed donkeys were also loaded with cracked and leaky wineskins, their stitches all coming undone. Some had been repaired a dozen times in clumsy ways.

And so a pathetic caravan was assembled, looking as if it had been on the dusty road for months and months.

With bold-faced audacity, these were now dispatched to go and meet with Joshua and his men. The ragged delegation would pretend in utter sincerity that they were bona fide emissaries sent from a far country. Yet in actual fact they came from a nearby community soon to fall under Joshua's forces.

Their tattered clothes, their worn-out sandals, their sad donkeys—skinny and bone weary—their stale, old bread along with cracked empty wineskins would convince the Israelis they had been weeks and weeks on the road. So when they sued for peace and offered to form an alliance, their statements would be believed. All the physical evidence was there to prove that they were ambassadors from a distant realm.

At first Joshua and his leaders were less than convinced. Somehow they were a bit suspicious that this was a trick to trap them. Point blank the rag-tag mob were grilled as to who they were and where they came from. After all, the deception and duplicity of the Canaanites was well-known. Lying, cheating, blatant dishonesty were all a way of life with the Semitic people of the Middle East. It has always been so. Consequently Joshua was not at all sure their story was true.

He was actually very unsure and suspicious of their statements.

Yet, at this point he faltered. He failed to seek the counsel and wisdom of God. He neglected to get clear guidance as to the decision he should make in dealing with these strangers.

With the obvious advantage of our hindsight it is rather simple for us to state, "When in doubt—don't!" But neither we nor Joshua always heed such wise advice. So inevitably there come times when we make decisions that turn out to be very damaging.

And this proved to be the case here. Joshua and his men believed the deception. They sat and listened to the long story of those who came to beguile them. Most surprising, they even lowered themselves to partake of their decomposing provisions.

This action impresses one as being totally at variance with the conduct of Israel now enjoying a land abundant in fresh fruit, delicious grains and bountiful livestock. The question may very well be asked, "Why would Joshua and his captains even deign to touch the moldy old bread, the fermented wine or other putrifying provisions of the fake Gibeonites?"

Even during all of their forty dreadful years in the dreary wilderness Israel had been so sustained by Jehovah that their clothes never became threadbare; their shoes never wore out; their rations never ran out. So for them to be so readily deluded by these visiting impostors strikes one as being inappropriate to a people ostensibly guided by God.

In fact it was! The whole ruse on the part of Gibeon was carried out successfully for two simple reasons. The first was the failure of Joshua and his officers to seek the mind of God in the matter. The second was to even consider an alliance with any foreign group, when already they had been specifically instructed to destroy all the occupants of Canaan.

The result was that Israel's commanders, completely beguiled by the visiting beggars, formed an association with them, whereby they were granted guarantees of peace and safety. Perhaps Joshua was moved to do this out of a certain sense of compassion. Or he may even have been convinced of their authenticity by their willingness to capitulate to Israel without a battle, surrendering themselves as servants to the invaders without any show of force.

Whatever the reason, the alliance was a mistake!

Within three days the truth was out. The impostors were none other than Gibeonites, occupants of nearby cities, which otherwise would have been the next to fall to Israel's forces.

Surprising as it seems, it was the common people of Israel, the laity so to speak, who this time rose up in anger and protest against their captains for the betrayal. They were a people who had tasted victory and conquest at both Jericho and Ai. Why should they be duped this way? Why should they be denied the flush of triumph and the spoils of war by their gullible commanders?

When they advanced against the adjacent towns of the Gibeonites, it was only to find that they had no choice but to come to terms with the occupants and grant them safe haven. It was akin to snatching a prey from the jaws of a powerful predator. So Israel's anger was roused to white fury.

Joshua, caught upon the twin horns of a desperate dilemma, at least had courage enough to carry out his commitments to the crafty Gibeonites. He had made a peace pact with them. They would not be injured or attacked. His word of surety would be honored. The enemy now in their midst would be protected. But it was as if Israel had made itself vulnerable to a quisling force within its widening new boundaries.

To keep this from becoming a major disaster, Joshua commanded that all the Gibeonites be brought into total bondage to Israel. They would, in fact, become as good as captives, slaves to their conquerors. Their forced labor was to be used to hew wood and bear water as serfs.

If the Gibeonites entertained any false illusions about remaining a free people in the company of Israel, they were quickly dashed to pieces. For Joshua placed an ominous curse and onerous burden of bondage on the impostors. They had sued for peace at any price. That peace would be paid for out of the sweat of their slavery from generation to generation.

Their dignity as a people would be preserved to some small degree in the specific labor to which they were assigned. Most of their work was to provide fuel and water for the priesthood who carried out all the sacrificial ceremonies in the tabernacle.

So it was that Israel, a nation of slaves who had been freed from the brickyards of Egypt, now found themselves in the ignoble role and insidious position of becoming slave masters. It had never been God's intention for this to happen. Subsequent history was to demonstrate how binding and crippling was the compact made with Gibeon.

Four hundred years later, Saul, Israel's first king, decided in a rash move to destroy the Gibeonites who troubled him. The appalling consequence was that seven of his sons were put to death because of this action (see 2 Samuel 21:1–9).

The profound spiritual principle at work in all of this strange scenario is one which eludes many of God's people. Put in the famous, forthright words of Dr. G. Campbell Morgan it can be stated this way: "A false step taken by a Christian can be forgiven by God. But, you must live with the consequences the rest of your life."

Many people assume that once a wrong move has been made, all that is necessary to arrest its results is simply to confess the mistake and seek forgiveness from God. This action does bring cleansing from our wrongs. It does remove the burden of guilt. But the on-going principle of "sowing and reaping" remains. There continues to be the outworking of cause and effect. This explains why a Christian cannot, in honesty and sincerity, go out to sin deliberately. To do so is to pay a high price of pain and suffering as a consequence of misconduct, to both himself and Christ.

Joshua and his captains had failed to determine God's will in this matter. Then in direct disobedience they came to terms with their antagonists. The net result was grief with the Gibeonites from generation to generation.

The same applies to us. We make false moves. We come to faulty decisions. We are subverted by the craftiness of our society and cunning of our culture. We fall prey to the apparently harmless tempters who come to us in many disguises. The net result is to become weakened internally, bound into vulnerability.

It is a peril for our future that we dare to come to terms with the world around us. *"He who is a friend to the world is at enmity with God"* (see James 4:4).

As God's people we dare not form binding associations with those who do not know or love Christ. We must not be trapped into compacts with non-Christians. We cannot come to comfortable terms with a world system set in opposition to the ongoing purposes of our God. There are no happy alliances between us and the enemy.

If, in a moment of weakness or gullibility, we are ensnared by our antagonists, there can be repentance and restitution. Yet the outworking of the consequences can cause us grief to the end of our days. Only the generous grace of God can make up to us for our willful wrong moves; only His mercy restores the weary wasted years that come from our rash compromises with evil.

Joshua was trapped when he could have triumphed.

The same is too often true of us!

15

Victory upon Victory

JOSHUA'S ALLIANCE with Gibeon was the catalyst which quickly precipitated a major military action with the hill tribes occupying the high country west of the Jordan valley. As soon as it was learned that Gibeon had come to terms with Israel and sued for peace, the anger and animosity of their old Canaanite confederates was aroused against them.

It was true the mountain kings had been terrified by the incredible reports of the invaders crossing the Jordan on dry ground. At first their will to wage war against Israel had drained away like spilled water when they heard that both Jericho and Ai had been utterly overrun and leveled by Joshua's forces.

Yet they were not reluctant to launch an attack of retribution on Gibeon as chastisement for joining themselves to the enemy. Gibeon was one of the Amorites' great royal cities. So it was unthinkable that they should side so readily with the Israelis.

It was Adonizedec, king of Jerusalem, who initiated this disciplinary action. He dispatched emissaries to Hoham king of Hebron, Piram king of Jarmuth, Japhia king of Lachish and

Debir king of Eglon inviting them to join him in battle against Gibeon, whom he felt confident could easily be overcome.

The five kings were quick to join forces. In a swift military maneuver they swept down out of the hills and encamped around Gibeon. The unexpected attack took the Gibeonites by surprise. Their former friends had suddenly become implacable foes. What was even more terrifying, they were outnumbered about five to one.

In utter fear an appeal for help was sent to Joshua, now encamped back at Gilgal on the banks of the Jordan. If the Gibeonites were to be spared from utter annihilation it would have to be with the formidable might of the Israeli forces. Nor was Gibeon too proud to press for this help from Israel.

Of course, from a purely military standpoint, this sudden outbreak of civil war amongst the Amorites was a tremendous tactical advantage for Joshua. One of the great basic strategies of any war is "to divide and conquer the enemy." Now in the providential arrangements of the Almighty, that was exactly what was happening here.

Again it is a classic demonstration to us of the remarkable manner in which God can take our grievous mistakes and bring benefit out of them for us. Because He is omnipotent, all wise, magnificent in mercy to His own, He turns our poor choices into magnificent opportunities to overcome. This concept is stated in a rather more formal way in the New Testament:

"And we know that all things
work together for good
to them that love God,
to them who are the called
according to his purpose" (Romans 8:28).

Joshua's willingness to immediately come to Gibeon's aid is a clear indication of the man's unusual and noble character. Most commanders in his position, seeing that Gibeon was under attack from her former allies, would have left her to perish.

This would have been considered just retribution for their deception and intrigue against Israel.

But Joshua was not of that ilk. He was not a man given to vengeance and spite. He was a leader who stood by his word. He had formed a peace pact with Gibeon. He would see to it that this treaty was honored and his name respected throughout the Middle East.

To take his men into action against the combined forces of the five mountain kings was the most formidable challenge he had ever faced. It was not the sort of engagement one entered with impunity. This would prove to be the pivotal point upon which the final conquest of all of Palestine would turn.

To his great credit Joshua never flinched. He never hesitated an hour. His response to Gibeon's call for help was immediate. So he set off at once, making a forced march across country in the dark of night.

To confirm his action, the Lord Jehovah came to Joshua with encouragement and enthusiasm. As of old the assurance was: "Fear them not: For I have delivered them into thine hand; there shall not a man of them stand before thee" (Joshua 10:18).

That exhilarating commitment was exactly what Joshua needed in this crisis. He and his men were facing formidable odds. And before the battles of the next few days were ended the Israelis would have fought over a far-flung range of enemy territory totally foreign to them. Like wide ranging hounds hot in the hunt they would pursue and slaughter the Canaanites all across the rough broken country of southern Palestine.

It would be a "blitzkrieg" type of combat. The conquest and annihilation of the five federated kings was a far cry from the careful encirclement of cities as had been the case with Jericho and Ai. Here the rampaging Israelis would sweep across the countryside in a mighty wave of force that left the enemy beaten and subdued. It was as if the irresistible tide of God's presence and power flooding over Canaan left its inhabitants powerless to defend themselves. All they could do was flee in wild disorder, only to be cut down and destroyed by the rampaging invaders.

But before any of this could occur, it was imperative for Joshua to believe implicitly in God's guarantee to achieve it. He was a man susceptible to foreboding just as we so often are. Without question there were occasions when the odds against him looked formidable. No doubt there were times when he, too, was gripped with cold terror.

Yet, amid all of this, Joshua's remarkable resilience lay in his quiet faith in God. He came to count on the reliability of the Almighty with calm confidence. He discovered that the resources of God were available to him as he appropriated them.

It is proper for us to see that in the life of God's people, faith and fear become mutually exclusive (fear here referring to anxiety and foreboding about the future).

"For God hath not given us the spirit of fear; but of power, and of love, and of a sound mind" (2 Timothy 1:7).

As we examine Joshua's courageous action we can only conclude that in magnificent measure he was a man imbued with the Spirit of the Living God. Not only did he move ahead with enormous confidence and courage, but also with a distinct concern for his new associates, the crafty Gibeonites. Above and beyond all his generosity and valor were the godly attributes of an unusually wise leader, who in years to come would be respected all across this region.

Too often Christians behave in ways which at first may seem brave and bold, yet lack the compassion, mercy, and wisdom of those led by God's Spirit. All three ingredients are essential to success—POWER, LOVE, and WISDOM—if we are to enjoy our Lord's blessing on our behavior.

Joshua's long night march to Gibeon took the enemy completely by surprise. The sudden appearance of the Israeli
forces overwhelmed the attackers from the hills. Already
alarmed by the reports of Israel's victories they fled in disarray,
hotly pursued by Joshua's warriors.

It was an exhilarating victory for Israel against great odds.
Up over the high country to the west they went like hounds hot
on the scent of a fleeing fox. They crossed the mountain passes
and pursued the routed foe on down past Makkedah and
Bethhoron.

Suddenly a furious thunderstorm blew up off the Mediterranean Sea. It swept into the hills, sending sheets of rain and a
storm of hailstones hurling down on the retreating Canaanites.
Their casualties from the cloudburst were incredible. For
when the Israelis came upon the dead and wounded they far
outnumbered those slaughtered by the swords and spears of
their own men. This divine intervention stirred Joshua's faith
to new heights.

He realized that to complete the rout of the Amorites his
forces would need more daylight hours. So in a bold act of
confidence in God he commanded that the sun should stand
still at its zenith and the moon should remain low on the
horizon.

Because of this extended day Israel was granted a glorious
victory over the enemy. In passing it may be noted that many
skeptics have been quick to discredit this historical event. Yet
the remarkable record has been validated by space scientists
who in calculating orbits around the outer planets of the sun
have invariably had to make meticulous allowance for this so
called "lost day."

The event demonstrated again the superb spiritual principle
that "God hearkens to the voice of a man who himself has
hearkened to the voice of God." It is in the initial crucible of
the overcomer's careful obedience to the Lord that He is
pleased to shape the conquests that later cover him with honor.

Miracle upon miracle was arranged by divine intervention in this engagement. Not only had there been a horrendous hailstorm, an amazing long day of full sunlight, but also the remarkable, sudden discovery that all five of the fabled mountain kings had chosen to "hole up" in the same highland cave near Makkedah.

Joshua ordered the great underground cavern sealed off with huge boulders. There the enemy leaders remained in mortal terror until the last of their fleeing forces had found refuge within their walled fortresses. Every other combatant had been annihilated as he tried to escape.

Joshua then returned to Makkedah and ordered the cave to be opened. The five trembling kings were brought out before him. They were ordered to prostrate themselves in the dust. Then Israel's commander had all of his gloating captains march past, each in turn placing his sandaled foot on the necks of the prostrate enemy war lords. This was a symbol of total victory. It was an affirmation of God's covenant with Israel that every place they set their foot down upon would be given to them in glorious conquest.

It was a moving moment in the long, sad history of this obstinate people. Never before had Israel been brought to such a pinnacle of power. Never before had her warriors tasted the heady wine of such a military triumph. Never before, in one fell swoop, had there been granted to this nonchalant nation such formidable momentum. In a single action five kings were wiped out.

Joshua himself drew his sword and slew the mountain monarchs. The five bodies were hung up in trees for all Israel to see what a victory they had achieved under God. When at last the long day was ended and the sun set to the west in the dim horizon of the blue Mediterranean, the bodies were taken down and entombed in the cave where the kings had been discovered.

But Israel's commander was not content with this astonishing conquest. He would not rest on his laurels. He was determined to make a clean sweep of all the south country from the Negev desert to Gaza on the coast and the high hills overlooking the Jordan to the east.

City after city, town after town, collapsed and tottered under attack. It was as if a ferocious and powerful predator had been let loose in the land. It was exactly as the two spies, Joshua and his friend Caleb, had declared forty years before when they stood bravely and shouted defiantly: *"These people are but bread for us"*—a prey to be captured and consumed.

Now that declaration of faith in God and certainty of victory over the high-walled cities of Canaan was coming to pass. In rapid, dazzling succession, day after day, seven cities collapsed under the lightning thrust of Joshua's advancing army. Makkedah, Libnah, Lachish, Gezer, Eglon, Hebron, and Debir fell like one domino after another in astonishing defeat and disarray.

It is important to realize that this total rout of the Canaanites was not just a purely military conquest for Israel. Rather it was a dual operation in which the power and influence of God Himself was actively at work within the walls of these fortified communities. Just as in the case of Jericho, the local residents of these mountain redoubts knew full well of Joshua's exploits. To a large extent their morale had been utterly broken before ever their cities were besieged.

It was a classic demonstration of the Lord's faithfulness to those who would follow Him unflinchingly. He had shown Himself mighty on behalf of those who obeyed His commands completely. To use the terminology of the Scriptural record, "The Lord delivered them [the enemy] into the hand of Israel" (Joshua 11:8).

God had brought Joshua and his people into Canaan. God had gone ahead by His Spirit to prepare the path for certain conquest. God had worked actively behind the scenes to demoralize the Amorites within their walled towns. Now God had granted Israel tremendous courage and energy to attack the enemy forces. God had performed miracles in the midst of combat. Now God had given glorious victories beyond their highest hopes.

All of His promises to His people had been performed.

He had shown Himself utterly trustworthy.

He demonstrated that He could deliver.

The net result was that within a matter of days Joshua had taken over an immense territory embracing roughly one third of the Promised Land. Few campaigns in military history could ever match this one under God's supreme strategy.

Joshua's honor, reputation and prestige as a brilliant commander were firmly established all across the Middle East. But most important was the affirmation that it was the Almighty God, Jehovah Himself, who had fought for His people.

It should still our spirits, stir our souls, and fire our own faith to realize that this same living Lord—the Risen Christ—by His Spirit stands ready to help us overcome today, just as of old, if we will but cooperate with Him in quiet obedience and calm confidence. He has not changed across the long centuries of human history!

16

The Long Campaign of Conquest

ALTHOUGH JOSHUA had achieved stunning victories over the Canaanites during the first few weeks of his invasion of their territory, it would require seven years to fully occupy and consolidate Israel's claims to all of the Promised Land. Remarkable and as far-ranging as this military conquest was, its horrendous history is summarized briefly in just one chapter of the scriptural account.

Few people today fully understand or comprehend the total extent of the territory taken over by this well-nigh invincible army. Their brilliant achievements against the most formidable odds are seldom given the honor and esteem they deserve.

This is doubly so when we pause to consider that in comparison with their adversaries, the Israelis were few in number, scarcely trained for war, and poorly equipped to wage any sort of protracted campaign. Yet, quite obviously, what they lacked in material advantages was more than made up for by the presence and power of Jehovah who so often intervened on their behalf in battle.

Not only did the Lord God endow Joshua with an unusual element of wisdom during the war of occupation, but even more important He bestowed on him incredible acumen in executing brilliant strategy far beyond his own devising. He became a military genius whose tactics enabled his fighting forces to take territory out of all proportion to their rather small numbers.

In addition to all of this Joshua was a commander, who, though he had made one or two errors, first at Ai, then with the Gibeonite alliance, was not deterred by them. Filled with enormous courage from God, exhilarated by his own fearless faith in the Most High, he charged and stimulated his forces with the same enormous assurance of victory.

He was God's man, moving under God's command, to achieve all the aims and aspirations of Jehovah for his people. He was not a self-deluded leader gloating over his own egocentric ambitions.

Because Joshua was so bold under God, his name and exploits became a terror to all the tribes of Palestine. In fear for their lives, and in a desperate last effort to survive, the various kingdoms joined forces in a grand alliance to counterattack the Israelis. But it would all be to no avail. For the promises and commitments made by God to Israel when first He brought them out of Egypt were to be executed in tremendous triumph.

Here were those assurances:
1) God's Angel would go before them into battle.
2) There would be no sickness amongst them.
3) Their herds and flocks would flourish.
4) An unnerving fear of the Lord would come upon all their enemies.
5) In panic their foes would turn their backs and flee before Israel.
6) Swarms of hornets would attack the occupants.
7) And so, steadily, surely, the Amorites, Hittites, Per-

izzites, Canaanites, Hivites and Jebusites would be cut off.
Not in one year, or two, but over a protracted period of time
(Exodus 23:20–33).

   As for Israel, her keys to success were clear:
1) Simply obey the commands of God.
2) Reject any overtures of peace from the enemy.
3) Abstain from any form of worship to their false gods.
4) Refuse to intermarry with any of the local inhabitants, all
of whom were to be annihilated.

On the surface this may have appeared to be a rather
straightforward arrangement. In actual fact it proved to be an
ongoing source of enticement to Israel. Only Joshua's strong
character and commanding presence kept his people from fall-
ing prey to the enemy.

   When the northern kingdoms joined forces to counterattack
Israel, Joshua was immediately confronted with a new, overwhelming element in battle. This was the marshalling of
masses of cavalry, composed of fierce combat units with horses
and chariots. These gave the Canaanites a tremendous military
superiority. Horsemen and chariots provided enormous mo-
bility which Israel did not possess. Also, the very sight of thundering war chariots bearing armed men into battle was enough
to intimidate the most valiant foot soldier.

   A lesser leader than Joshua would have blanched with fear at
the prospect of closing battle with such superior forces. As far
as the eye could see masses of men, horses, and chariots assembled near the headwaters of the Jordan. The area was
known as "The Waters of Mirom" where a small open lake,
about three miles by two miles in extent, stood shining in the
sun.

   Virtually no details are given of this engagement. It may
very well have been one of the most violent and bloody battles
during the entire occupation.

All we are told is that the Lord reassured Joshua, as of old, that he was not to be apprehensive. He was not to be intimidated by the seething masses of the enemy whose shining weapons and glinting chariots sparkled on the plain like grains of sand upon the seashore. This was a new form of war, but it was a war God would wage. For within twenty-four hours the enemy warriors in uncounted thousands would be slain by the hand of the Almighty.

All that would remain would be the unmanned horses and chariots. In utter panic and pandemonium the uncontrolled cavalry units would be rushing in every direction without riders or charioteers. The cruel chariot wheels and plunging hooves would be crushing the corpses and mutilating the bodies of the dead. The ground would be soaked red with blood from the carnage.

Israel's fighting men did not even have to stand against a cavalry charge. Instead they had the grisly assignment to hamstring all the horses, put them to death, and set the torch to all the elaborate chariots of war.

This may have seemed an absurd waste for an army that up until now had no cavalry units of its own. The normal, natural inclination might have been to seize the horses and chariots as prizes of war, to be turned to Israel's great advantage in future engagements. But it was not to be. God's command to Joshua was one of total annihilation. This he carried out in absolute compliance with divine direction.

The amazing result of this incredible triumph was that Joshua's men swept not only as far as Sidon on the Mediterranean coast, they also then moved eastward across the Jordan valley into the wild regions of the trans-Jordan deserts.

By his bold action Joshua demonstrated that he was a man on the move for God. He was not reluctant to accept any new challenge that confronted him. Whatever unexpected and foreign force he faced, he would tackle it with calm courage and fearless faith. He convinced all those under his command that "one man with God is invincible." By his actions and by his implicit compliance with God's word to him he was able to achieve overwhelming victory. This was faith in action.

This engagement with the Canaanite cavalry units was much more than a military maneuver. It was also a decidedly spiritual conquest. It displayed Joshua's determination not to rest on his laurels, not to bask in the glow of past achievements, nor to settle for less than the total achievement of every objective set before him by God.

As Christians we would do well to emulate this man's character and conduct in our walk with Christ. We should not fear change. We need not flinch from forbidding challenges. We dare not draw back when the way opens for us to advance. As ever of old, Christ keeps company with His people. He goes before us. He prepares a way. He overcomes the opposition. He causes us to triumph. He enables us to gain new ground.

Let us just have the grit to go on with Him.

God will grant us some glorious conquests.

This startling victory over the northern kingdoms was fully equal to Joshua's triumph over the southern confederation. There now remained the rather tedious, meticulous task of mopping up town after town that remained entrenched behind their high fortress walls. One by one in steady succession Israel besieged the enemy enclaves. It was Jehovah's eternal intention that all of Canaan be swept clear and clean of its pagan occupants.

There was no doubt of the constant temptation present for the victorious Israelis to settle down comfortably in the areas occupied. It may have seemed so pleasant to stake out pastures, fields, orchards and villages for themselves. But this was not God's immediate intention for them. They were an invader on the move. They were a military force in action. And their ultimate objective was to sweep all of Palestine clear of all its residents. None, absolutely none, were to remain.

The main reason for this severe and stern extermination of the enemy was this: God knew full well any who survived would pose a perpetual threat to Israel. The insidious idolatry of the Canaanites, their pagan moral perversion, their cruel and crass culture could all contaminate and corrupt His chosen people. Joshua understood this danger. Nor was he about to let it subvert those under his command.

It will be recalled that not only was the word of God to him that he be a military leader to Israel, but also a shepherd in charge of their spiritual well-being. And this he was determined to do at any cost. He simply would not stand by and see Israel perverted and polluted by the people they conquered. To do so would be to have triumph turn into grievous tragedy.

He took the chain of command established from God to Moses to himself very seriously. Whatever had been ordained of the Lord he was determined to do. His highest priority was to carry out his divine assignments.

The remarkable record of these years, left to all of us, is that Joshua took all the land needed to accommodate Israel. He occupied all the valleys, all the plains, all the Mediterranean coast, all the Jordan region, all the hill country as far north as Lebanon, all the southern arid wastes as far as the Negev desert. It was a stupendous achievement that went on without letup year after year with success following on success.

Even more astonishing is the amazing commendation left to us in this inspired report: "Joshua left nothing undone of all that the Lord commanded Moses."

What a record!

What an accolade!

What an accomplishment!

How many of us could claim such an achievement?

There is a simplicity, a brevity, a matter-of-fact element in this historical narrative that belies all of the grandeur of this gallant man of God. He stands out in Israel's story as a towering person of power and prominence that eclipses his contemporaries. And the reason for this probably escapes the reader. *Because it was Joshua himself who narrated and reported the stupendous events of his era.*

He makes no attempt to cover his own conduct with glory. He does not succumb to the temptation to gild his own character. Rather, in simple facts he reports how he discharged his duty to the Most High.

In all the annals of human history, this surely must be one of the most spartan yet sublime records left to us of a man who lived for only one thing: *To do God's will!* Of all God's basic commands to him, he left nothing undone.

Little wonder that the little nation of Israel, under his fearless command, took such an immense territory. Little marvel that they put to rout the enemy so strongly entrenched in their strong cities. Little surprise that they swept away their kings, wiped out their forces and laid claim to all their cattle, sheep and crops.

It mattered not who stood against them. Even the fearsome, huge giants, the Anakim, were hapless before Joshua and his men. Where forty years before his associates claimed they felt like "grasshoppers" before such stalwarts, now Joshua trod them down underfoot like so much stubble in an autumn harvest field.

In stubbornness and willfulness none of the enemy tribes, apart from the Gibeonites, had tried to come to terms with Joshua. Each in desperate determination fought the invaders for survival. Yet each in turn fell under the ferocious onslaught of the Israelis. This long war lasted at least seven full years, longer than either World War of the twentieth century.

It was a campaign of remorseless attrition against the Canaanites. Finally it was brought to a victorious conclusion. Joshua had gained sufficient ground to give all of Israel a rich and bountiful inheritance as ordained of God. Combined with this he now ushered in an era of peace, prosperity and rest for his people.

All of this has been rather easy and simple to describe with pen and paper. But for Joshua and his followers it entailed long years of remarkable fortitude and courage. It called for faith in God. It demanded coming into direct combat with the enemy again and again.

The lessons inherent in the character and conduct of this man are so obvious they need little elaboration here. Yet the basic spiritual principles which undergirded his success need to be clearly stated.

1) Let us always be ready to accept any new challenge given to us under God. Let us keep on the move with Him. Do not stagnate spiritually. Be bold enough to take new territory with Christ.

2) Leave nothing undone which Christ commands us to do. Let us be diligent, earnest, and thorough in any assignment He gives us. There must be no shirking of our responsibilities to Him and others.

3) No matter how awesome the "giants" in our experience, He can enable us to conquer them. And in His own good time, in His own generous way, He will grant us that inner rest which is the rightful heritage of His people.

17

The Partition of the
Promised Land

THE SUBJUGATION of Canaan had seen the total defeat of some
thirty-one so-called kings, along with their little kingdoms.
Year by year, bit by bit, one monarchy after another had fallen
under Joshua's relentless attack. Only here and there some
resolute enclave of the enemy would hold out and refuse to
capitulate completely to the Israeli forces.

It had not been an easy campaign. It took its toll of Joshua's
formidable strength. Though he was a man of remarkable
stamina, the steady strain of combat and war began to leave its
mark upon the commander. Most leaders would have suc-
cumbed far sooner, but Joshua was determined he would see
God's purposes for His people accomplished in Canaan.

Joshua realized that despite his valiant conquests, despite
the blood-tingling victories, despite the large area now under
his control, there remained much land still to be possessed.
But for the present it appeared imperative that he should proceed to partition the territory among the tribes of Israel.

This was no easy thing to do. Rivalry, jealousy and the never-
ending jostling for advantage were all part of the difficulties

which would have to be surmounted. Little wonder it was so imperative that God should grant him a special endowment of wisdom for this delicate diplomatic assignment.

For, even though he was an aged veteran, held in high esteem by his contemporaries, Joshua knew full well of the hidden anger and bitter animosity that could erupt if his division of the land was not deemed fair. Even if he had been so triumphant as a military commander, it did not necessarily imply that he would be as successful in the political arena of partitioning land to such petulant people.

Still, this was a responsibility entrusted to him by Jehovah God. He was not about to back away from the challenge or cringe from the demands upon his waning vitality. He would face this task, too, with fearless faith.

There are principles played out for us here in this partition of the territory which must not be overlooked. First is the fact that this was a task given to an older man of wide experience. Great respect and reverence were rendered to the aged commander. His experience, his wisdom, his prudence, his maturity, his spiritual stature, his objectivity, his lack of desire for personal gain were attributes recognized and honored by his associates.

This is not the case in our culture. Too often there is the tendency among North Americans to idolize and adore youth. The elderly are often shoved to the side, even ignored, spurned as though they were burned out, "spent candles." This should not be the case among Christians. Numerous admonitions are given in God's Word to honor and respect the elderly among us.

Second, from the standpoint of the senior himself, there needs to be the unquenchable fire within to press on for God. There should be an acute awareness that it is a challenge from God Himself to undertake new tasks and achieve new goals.

This is not to indulge in some brash act of bravado far beyond our ability. But rather it is to step out boldly with our Father's strength and direction to do His bidding.

Advanced age is not a period in life for pantomime. It is not the time for theatrics or silly showmanship to try and prove one's prowess. But it is an opportunity to show the faithfulness of our Father in sustaining us in His service.

"O God, thou hast taught me from my youth:
and hitherto have I declared thy wondrous works.
Now also when I am old and greyheaded,
O God, forsake me not; until I have shewed
thy strength unto this generation,
and thy power to every one that is to come"
(Psalm 71:17–18).

The Almighty had granted to Joshua enormous victory. He had bestowed on him triumph upon triumph in taking new territory. He had endowed him with a resplendent legacy of honor, prestige and power throughout all of Palestine.

But it was not intended ever to be only his, for his own personal self-gratification. Rather, this remarkable legacy of land was entrusted to Joshua to be shared fairly with all of his fellow Israelis. The very fact that Joshua was never ever corrupted by the power and influence put within his grasp is a mark of the sterling character of this magnificent man. Any lesser leader would have been tempted to abuse and misuse his position.

The main secret of Joshua's outstanding behavior was the utter loyalty he showed in submitting to the divine chain of command established by God. In a sense it really was Jehovah who would divide the terrain. His will and His wishes would be ascertained by Eleazer the high priest.

Acting under the unction of Urim, the spiritual leader in

Israel would determine with both justice and righteousness which portion of the country fell to each tribe. So it is appropriate to say that Joshua's role was that of a "man under command" to God. His responsibility was to see that God's wishes for Israel were carried out in His own appointed way. He it was who must lead Israel to understand that as each lot was drawn, the legacy so arranged was God's plan and not a man's.

Of course this relieved Joshua of being blamed for any injustice. But most important it helped Israel to recognize their unique form of social government under God. Unlike the thirty-one miniature monarchies which had been supplanted, Israel was essentially a theocracy under the direct sovereignty of Jehovah God.

The remarkable result was that the division of Canaan among the eleven tribes proceeded without wrangling, angry disputes or jealous recrimination. This in itself stands as one of the most monumental land settlements in human history. That it could be achieved so swiftly and so amicably is an enduring monument to Joshua's integrity.

The twelfth tribe, the tribe of Levi, from whom the priests were drawn, did not inherit territory as such. It was the duty of the entire nation to subscribe to their support through their tithes and sacrificial offerings (see Numbers 18:20–21).

As God had stated to Moses, He Himself was to be Levi's inheritance and provider. He it was who would care for them. Still, in due course special cities would be set aside in which they resided among the rest of the nation as the spiritual servants of the Most High.

Through all of this complex transaction there runs the silver thread of a grand, old, gray-headed general quietly but firmly establishing all of his countrymen in the exact place of their appointment under God. He it was who in a practical way as their spiritual shepherd had led Israel out of the wilderness wastes into the bounty and abundance of their Promised Land.

Now each tribe was given its own special ground ordained and arranged of God. At last they were "home." At last they could "put down roots." At last they could relish the "rest of the righteous."

It is likewise our Father's intention that the same be true of us today. We are not here to build our own private kingdoms. We are not granted rich legacies from the Lord to lavish on ourselves. We do not inherit His riches just to squander them on selfish impulses.

We are like Joshua, stewards of the Most High, entrusted with enormous benefits from above which it is our responsibility to share gladly with others. We are here to dispense the largesse of heaven with our generation that they too be enriched as we are. Freely we have received. Freely then let us give . . . gladly, generously.

It was during this partition of the country that Caleb, Joshua's sturdy and loyal companion, came to his leader to lay personal claim to Mount Hebron as his own special property. This had been promised to him as a private legacy by Moses.

This was the land over which he had traveled when he and Joshua were sent in as spies more than forty years previously. It was terrain upon which he had set his feet in a positive act of faith claiming it from the enemy under God's great hand. Now he wished to take title to it as it were. He had waited more than forty-five years for this hour. The time for settlement had come.

Caleb took no credit to himself for his long life and sturdy endurance. He knew full well that it was the generous care and strong protection of God Himself which had sustained him all these years. Still, on the other hand, he could declare unflinchingly before Joshua and his other comrades in arms, "I wholly followed the LORD my God" (Joshua 14:8).

When his compatriots had rebelled against the Lord, only

Joshua and Caleb had the courage to stand for Him. When Israel demanded a new leader to replace Moses, who would take them back into the atrocious bondage of Egypt, it was Caleb and Joshua who defiantly dared to challenge the chanting mob to take God's side. Even at risk of being stoned to death, these two fearless warriors shouted boldly, "God will go before us! God will drive out the enemy! God will give us the land of promise!"

For more than forty years both these stalwarts had clung to this trust in God tenaciously. Now at last all of Jehovah's commitments to them had been fully vindicated. The promises made to His people had all been performed. The assurances given to Israel had been accomplished just as the Most High had declared.

Caleb was unashamed to claim his inheritance. It was his by virtue of Moses' promise to him. It was his by right of God's commitment to him. It was his, because on his part he had fulfilled all his commitments to the Lord in total obedience.

Using terminology familiar to an older generation, we can put it this way: "Caleb was possessing his possessions!" This he did forthrightly and fearlessly.

This was a remarkable act of confidence in God. The more so when we pause to appraise what it actually was Caleb wanted. He was not, in his old age and advancing years, seeking a soft spot or comfortable little corner of the country to settle in. No, no, no! Instead the tough, grizzled, old war horse was prepared to take a whole rugged mountain range for himself. It was the stronghold of the sons of the ferocious giants of the Anakim.

That was no deterrent to doughty Caleb. He was not a man to shrivel up in fear at this late stage of his life. "Give me the mountain!" he chortled in an outburst of triumph. "As my strength was before, for war, so it is now, undiminished, able to go out and come in at will!" He grinned with glee, a look of victory already glimmering in his blazing eyes—"God will be with me as He said, and I shall be able to drive out the enemy giants!"

Such courage! Such confidence! Such calmness! It was the stuff from which great ambitions and mighty exploits are woven in a man's walk with God. The stirring audacity of his friend and comrade in arms for over forty years thrilled and stimulated Joshua. What an uplift and inspiration to have this lion of a warrior alongside him.

Joyously, gratefully, Joshua granted Caleb his request. "Go, Caleb, go! Mount Hebron is yours! Storm the heights! Scatter the enemy to the winds! Take the territory which God has given to you. You have set down your feet in faith. Now rejoice in the rightful inheritance which is yours under God. You will find respite and rest from war."

And this is exactly what Caleb did. Not only did he lay claim to, and conquer, all of Mount Hebron which means, "I have crossed over," but subsequently, with help from others, subjugated all the southern regions of the Negev desert. These he bequeathed to his daughter Achsah, and the brave young man who gained her hand in combat with Caleb against the giants.

These southern regions being a dry and desperate desert, Achsah requested from her father both lower and upper springs in order to water her herds and flocks. Caleb complied with her wishes, sharing the abundance he possessed in the high country. It was a generous gesture identical to the remarkable partition of the land given to all of Israel by Joshua, who never once claimed the lion's share for himself, as most military commanders might have done.

The gracious and magnanimous conduct of Caleb and Joshua was a reflection of their sterling characters. Here were mighty men of fearless faith in God. Even with advanced age their desire to achieve great exploits for God never waned. Their willingness to wage relentless war against the enemy never diminished. Their unflinching confidence in the Most High to grant them rest at last never flagged. They were stalwarts to the end of their days with flags flying.

Their example should stir all of us to noble aims and heady exploits for Christ. We all can claim our mountains from God: move out against the enemy with faith; gain new and higher ground; never rest until all the terrain is taken; share gladly what we have!

Unfortunately and unhappily, in a small footnote of sober contrast, the report is made of this period that this never happened to Jerusalem. Israel never did fully subdue this mountain town. Its inhabitants, the Jebusites, never were completely conquered. Like a cancerous tumor this bit of territory remained to infect Israel down to this very day.

Nor will its tragic malignancy ever end until the ultimate conclusion of human history. Even at this hour the Arab world looks upon the "the dome of the rock" in the heart of Jerusalem as one of their most sacred shrines. Yet it is in a city claimed by Israel to be their own rightful capitol. What an enigma!

18

Joshua Takes His Own Mountain

STRANGE AS IT may seem, the only dispute ever to erupt over
the settlement of the Promised Land had to do with Ephraim
and Manasseh. These two tribes descended from Joseph, the
favored son of Jacob. This man had become prime minister of
Egypt under the rule of the Pharaohs. At his death, he skillfully
crossed his arms in blessing his boys. So the greater portion of
the inheritance fell upon Ephraim the younger, rather than
Manasseh the older.

Through the ensuing centuries these two tribes became no-
toriously powerful and aggressive in Israel. Ephraim, who inci-
dentally had always been represented by Joshua as their
chosen leader, was famous for its fighting men, while Manasseh was recognized as a tribe of ferocious warriors.

They now insisted that they be given a greater share of
Canaan. Because of their large numbers and formidable fighting forces they felt entitled to a better portion than had fallen to
them in their one lot.

Joshua, who himself was their long-respected leader, and
one of them, really did not dispute their claim. In a move of
wise diplomacy he endorsed their bravery in battle and greatness in numbers. He concurred with all their claims to fame.

Instead of allowing their contention for more land to degen-
erate into a diatribe against either himself, Eleazer, or even
God, he lifted their spirits up with a stirring challenge. "You
are a great people! You do have tremendous power! Go out and
seize the mountain ranges. Cut down the forests. Clear out the
giants. Claim the ground!"

This was a battle call to great exploits. But Joshua did not just
leave it at that. "Spread out your forces. Sweep down into the
plain of Jezreel. Defeat the Canaanites of the low country with
their chariots of iron. You can overpower the enemy!"

This was the sort of call to conquest that stirred the fighting
instincts of every man strong enough to swing a battle sword. It
was heady wine that excited the impulses of everyone who
hankered for a home and land of his own. Joshua's battle cry
was like an unfurled banner flying over their heads—the bugle
call to take enemy territory in fearless assault.

Nor was Joshua the sort of armchair commander content
with laying out strategy which others were ordered to carry out
while he reclined safely behind the lines in security. The challenge which he threw out to his fellow tribesmen he himself
was willing to pick up. He never held back. He was ever ready
to be in the forefront of combat.

In due time, when all other territorial claims had been settled, he requested for himself that he be given Timnath-Serah
in Mount Ephraim. The names alone of this terrain give us a
clear and thrilling insight into Joshua's expectations. Timhath-
Serah means "My abundant portion" and Mount Ephraim de-
notes "Where I shall be doubly fruitful."

Joshua was not a man to settle for mediocrity. He was not
content to bask in the afterglow of past conquests. He was not a
man to settle down softly in some cozy corner where he would
be corrupted by complacency.

This remarkable commander was keen to face new challenges in his own career. He was prepared to lay claim to fresh
high ground under God with his own faith. He was ready to

face the enemy and achieve personal exploits just as he had told others to do.

Never, ever, could it be said of Joshua that he was one who lived the double life of duplicity at which the onlooker scoffed and remarked with skepticism, "Just do what I say, but don't do as I do!"

Rather the short, stabbing, startling record given to us is that Joshua took Timnath-Serah. He cleared the high country. He established a city there. And that is where he chose to reside.

It is appropriate that we should pause here briefly to understand what is meant by all the adventures of Israel at this explosive point in her history. Respectfully I would remind the reader again of a statement made at the beginning of this book, namely, "The final triumphant entry into the land flowing with milk and honey is the victorious song of the soul that triumphs in Christ. It displays the overcoming life of the soul set free from self, finding its fulfillment and rest in the place of God's provision."

This was now true of Israel as a people.

It was likewise true of Joshua as a man.

Both collectively and privately there was victory.

This is always God's intention for His people. It has always been His keenest desire for us as individuals. It is His ultimate purpose for us.

Christ calls us to be overcomers. He challenges us to great conquests both in the church as a whole as well as in our private lives. His vision always is that we should be victors.

Above and beyond all the battles and struggles it is His ultimate purpose that we be those who not only take territory but occupy it to find fruitful lives rich in the abundance of His provision.

In contrast to all of this the church so often appears to be embattled. It seems at best to be in a stale and sterile "holding pattern." Instead of storming the enemy strongholds it stands still as if under siege itself. This has never been our Lord's intention.

When He was here among us He declared fearlessly: *"The gates of hell shall not prevail* (be able to stand) *against the assault of the church."* We, like Israel of old, should be storming the enemy strongholds. We should be laying claim to all their redoubts. We should be forcing the very gates of enemy-held territory, tearing down the walls of opposition, surmounting the forces against us.

Too long now the church has been on the defensive. Too long she has been anything but a "terrible army with flags flying—advancing under the battle colors of the Most High."

What is true of the church collectively, is likewise true of so many Christians privately. Their lives are a dreary round of defeat, despair and depression. Millions of man-hours are spent by pastors and preachers applying poultices to pathetic people wallowing in self-pity. Instead of challenging their congregations to get moving for God, to take territory with Christ, to sense the sweeping surge of God's Holy Spirit leading on to conquest, they treat their people like so many emotional invalids.

All sorts of counseling centers are set up to serve neurotic cripples. Books, pamphlets and seminars are provided to pamper pathetic people bogged down in defeat and despair. The world's ways and the world's techniques and the world's prescriptions are used to try and remedy the creeping impotence among Christians.

It is amazing indeed to see the forebearance of God amid such mundane and miserable performances. His patience with perverse people today is no less than it was in the days of Israel in the desert.

He calls all of us away from despair and defeat. Like Joshua at Timnath-Serah, Christ challenges us to enter new territory, to overcome the enemy, to clear the ground of our lives from the undergrowth of the world. He stirs us to seek higher ground, to enter into the rich, abundant life He offers, to find repose and contentment in Him.

This inner "rest" or "repose" for the Christian is a state of spiritual contentment which comes to those whose quiet confidence rests in God. It has nothing to do with so called "happiness" that depends upon what is happening around the Christian in his outer contacts with the world.

It was an integral part of Joshua's life. For the remainder of his long and illustrious career in Canaan, until the day of his death some forty years later, he was a sterling leader who had achieved and attained his reward in rest. Always, his single-minded determination to do only God's will and to serve His purposes produced this remarkable repose.

Too often Christians have not come to this place of rest in their relationship to the Lord. Far too many have never learned to fully trust God for victory in the conflicts of life. They have not yet been brought to the point where without hesitation they promptly, gladly, bravely obey His wishes in every situation. They still strive to solve their own dilemmas with their own human resources, rather than committing their difficulties to the care and solution of the Most High.

This "place of peace," this "state of inner serenity," this "rest of the righteous" does not imply that life for God's person is a tranquil trail exempt from trouble. No indeed. Our Savior stated flatly to His followers,

"In the world ye shall have tribulation: but be of good cheer: I have overcome the world" (John 16:33).

When our lives are lived in quiet, inner communion with God, when our strength and assurance repose in His presence with us, when our faith rests in His capacity to conquer and overcome all that assails us, we come to find rest in Him.

This is to be in harmony with Christ.

And it is a pleasure for Him to honor our faith with the joy and contentment of His companionship.

Such a soul becomes invincible in the midst of conflict.

This is the Christian who stands sturdy and serene amid all the surging struggles of his/her sojourn on earth.

Through the changing scenes of life, despite all disasters and difficulties, amid the confusion and complexity of human society, this overcomer reposes in the rich resources of God. He knows victory in Christ. He is serene in the power of God's gracious Spirit who resides with him.

It should be added here as an important footnote that the greatest single secret to finding this inner spiritual rest is humility of heart.

It is worthy of our close attention that Joshua was the very last in all of Israel to claim his rightful inheritance. He had every right to be the first. As the brilliant, victorious commander of his nation, he had brought not only himself great glory but also all his compatriots.

Yet, instead of insisting on prior place, instead of choosing his lot first, instead of demanding the right to select the best land for himself, he waited until last.

God always honors and exalts such an attitude!

Inevitably it turns out that the first shall be last, and the last shall be first. This is to be greatest in the divine economy of God. This is to be lifted up to a place of prominence and honor.

Joshua was not a man to glory in his own apparent success. He was not on any sort of ego trip. Nor did he ever indulge himself in any false impressions of self-importance. He was not half as concerned with "who he was" as with the thought of "whose he was." He had the profound spiritual insight to realize that all of his remarkable exploits were granted to him by God.

He knew—it was God who had promised Canaan to His people;

it was God who had given deliverance from the desert;

it was God who had guided them across Jordan;

156

it was God who had dismayed the enemy cities;
it was God who had fought for them in battle;
it was God who had given them great victories;
it was God who could now grant them prolonged
peace!

Another amazing aspect of Joshua's character and conduct
was that he never once showed any inclination to seize power
for his own selfish purposes. Unlike so many of Israel's leaders
in subsequent generations, he never hankered for self-exalta-
tion. He was not one to grasp for personal prestige or to use his
enormous exploits as stepping stones to private aggrandize-
ment. Power did not corrupt him. Nor did he overstep the
spiritual authority of Eleazer the high priest. Not once did he
attempt to usurp the prior place of Israel's spiritual leadership.

Whatever clear instructions came to him from God, he
promptly proceeded to carry them out with implicit obedience. This explains why it was possible for him and Eleazer
to partition the whole of Palestine with so little difficulty. It
explains why he could have all of the boundaries of every tribe
meticulously drawn, described and registered in an orderly
manner still used in real estate transactions to this very day. It
explains how specific cities, in which the Levites and their
families would reside, could be selected without wrangling or
dispute. It explains how they could have sufficient land around
them to provide for their family needs.

In every move he made Joshua demonstrated a degree of
wisdom and integrity seldom, if ever, matched in the troubled
history of the human race. All of us know all too well how
glorious victories in war are so often marred by the corrupt and
cruel partition of land after the conflict—a classic example
being the Yalta agreements after World War II that con-
demned most of Eastern Europe to the cruel tyranny of life
under political oppression.

There was none of this intrigue, folly or sinister motivation in Joshua. His character was above subversion. His conduct was impeccable. His compassion was remarkable.

All of this was clearly displayed in the establishment of cities of refuge to which innocent offenders could flee until fully acquitted. Here family feuds and explosive rivalries could be diffused in peace.

Not only was Joshua a mighty man of war, he was also a potent force for peace throughout all his generation!

19

Joshua's Wise Admonition
to His Warriors

THE WAR YEARS were over. The whole of the Promised Land
had been partitioned in peace. The spoils of war had been
seized and distributed with justice to all. It was time now for
the fighting men of Israel to return to their tents, to rejoin their
families, to settle down quietly, to establish their homes in
contentment.

Particularly was this true for the warriors from Reuben, Gad
and the half tribe of Manasseh who had been so active in the
campaign of conquest west of the Jordan. Now all the battle-
hardened men of war were summoned before Joshua. He was
dispersing them to their new homes. He was at last disbanding
the units that had fought so valiantly under his command. But
before their final departure the old veteran commander himself had some parting instructions for his comrades in arms.

He reminded them as always that it really was God Himself
who had gone before them into combat. He brought to their
attention that it was God who had routed the enemy in battle.
He reiterated for a last time that it was the Most High who had
fought on their behalf, granting them great victories and, now,
total rest from counterattack.

Because of all this Joshua went on to point out that Israel could now occupy their rightful inheritance without misgivings. As a people it was possible for them to quietly possess their promised possessions. At long last they were in a powerful position to enjoy their newly won land in security and strength. They could relish their new-found rest in a region of fruitful and abundant productivity.

Yet Joshua was wise enough to alert his men to the fact that this new life of serenity was not a life of ease. It demanded as much spiritual diligence to prosper in times of peace as it did to prevail in times of conflict.

Inspired by the Spirit of God given to him in abundant measure at the time of his commissioning, Joshua displayed an enormous degree of wisdom in his parting instructions. He set before his tough fighters the preconditions for living in peace and prosperity. Here they are. Nor have they altered in one iota down to this very day:

1) God it is who has granted us great benefits. In quiet humility, without fanfare or ostentation, let us lay hold of all that He places at our command. In forthright faith we are to reach out and take the territory granted to us. We are to claim in serene confidence the resources which He puts at our disposal.

This does not call for blatant displays of bravado. But it does demand that, by calm reliance on Christ, I trust Him implicitly to provide for me in abundant measure all that is needed to repose in rest.

2) As in war, so in the place of peace, it is imperative to comply precisely with the will and wishes of God. Simply because the pressures, dangers and risks of battle are absent, does not imply that the need to cooperate fully with God's commands has diminished or altered.

It demands no less diligence to carry out Christ's commands in the times of tranquillity than it does in the hours of hostilities. If anything more so, since our human tendency is to grow slack and indolent when things go well.

3) Our love for the Lord is not just a highly charged emotional state in which tremendous daring is displayed for God in the heat and danger of our battles. It is also that steady loyalty to Him displayed in a strong life of devotion and integrity amid our times of relaxation.

It has been well said that the true test of a man's character is what he does in his leisure hours. Many of us can demonstrate enormous heroism in the clash of conflict. It is often ease and plenty that perverts the best of people, and thus their love for God grows cold.

4) Joshua made it abundantly clear that just because the battles were behind them, the need to walk with God in peace still remained an absolute priority. Over and over the warriors had advanced against the enemy. They had marched around their cities. They had taken new and terrifying terrain by setting down one foot after the other with fearless faith in God.

What worked in war would likewise work in the place of peace. God's principle of power never altered because of circumstances. It takes as much faith to produce a crop of corn as it does to storm and seize an enemy stronghold. One must act in confidence, sure that God will play His part, whether in a cornfield or on a battlefield.

5) There would need to be a constant vigilance in their reverence and respect for the eternal edicts of the Most High—not only in the sense of being people who are ready to do His will and obey His commands, but in the more profound dimension of preserving the divine revelation given to us by God as to His own character and our own conduct.

Very often amid affluence, ease and relative peace, human beings tend to settle down softly and take their heritage very much for granted. What men will lay down their lives for in battle, is sometimes obscured and overlooked amid our opulence. Often truth itself is lost more readily in the lap of luxury than it ever is in the clash of battle. God's Word does not change whether our lives are in danger or in security.

6) Always, ever, an individual must cleave to Christ. Our strength reposes in Him. It is the Lord God Himself who causes us to conquer in our combat with the forces of evil. It is likewise He and He alone who by His constant companionship can impart to us contentment and serenity in the days of our rest.

We do not build our hope around our achievements, possessions, friends or families. Our confidence reposes in the remarkable presence of our God sharing all the events of our tranquil little lives with us.

7) Out of genuine gratitude and hearty appreciation to our Father for all of His benefits, we are motivated to serve Him as faithfully in peace as in war. We are overwhelmed by His gracious generosity. We are stabbed and startled wide awake by His gracious victories granted to us. We are acutely conscious that every gift and every beautiful benefit bestowed upon us comes ultimately from His great hands.

In our place of peace, then; in our times of tranquillity; in our days of delight we desire that His name be honored. In all of this we are moved to share our abundance with others, not to expend it only on ourselves. We are stimulated to serve our generation and bless our God with the bounties He has bestowed on us.

These were the cardinal secrets to success that Joshua shared with his comrades in arms. They were wise rules of personal conduct for anyone wishing to flourish and prosper in the days of their rest just as they had gloried in the days of their battles.

Admonished in this manner the warriors from Reuben, Gad and the half tribe of Manasseh took leave of Joshua. They had fought faithfully for their fellow Israelis. All of their obligations were fulfilled. At last they could return to their families and flocks in the rugged rangelands across the river.

On the way back they stopped to erect an altar on the banks of the Jordan. It was intended by them to be a memorial commemorating their part in the war of occupation. It was also intended as a reminder to their posterity that their fathers had earned a rightful share in the rich heritage of Israel under God.

Their action was misconstrued by those living west of Jordan. They saw it as a first step in a break away from Jehovah. As is so often common in human affairs it was basically a most grievous misunderstanding that very nearly precipitated a civil war between the two factions of Israel. Happily Eleazer's son was able to restore trust and understanding that led to peace being restored.

Quietly and gently the years rolled by. The people of Israel steadily settled down into their new inheritance. New homes, villages and communities were established. Fields were planted to grain, while groves of olives, figs and dates were set out. Vineyards were established. Forests were cleared to provide more range and grazing land for their increasing herds of livestock.

This nation under God had finally come into full possession of all that had been promised by the Most High. They were enjoying a level of affluence and productivity that enabled them to become a wealthy and powerful people amid all of their abundant prosperity.

Joshua, as their leader, had achieved success not only for himself, but he had also brought all of Israel into a possession of remarkable resources. He had succeeded, as very few rulers ever do, in establishing a state where all of its citizens shared in its benefits and bounties.

Yet the secret to this unusual success was the basic fact that Israel was in essence a theocracy, not a democracy or a dictatorship. Joshua never fell prey to the temptation of becoming either a powerful political figure or of assuming the flagrant role of a royal sovereign.

Lesser, weaker, contriving men might have done this to promote their own ends. But not Joshua. He had the profound spiritual insight to see clearly that it was only Jehovah who was truly Israel's Sovereign. It was only God Himself who was truly worthy of their allegiance. It was the Lord who had delivered them from Egypt and brought them into this bountiful land. So it was imperative for Israel to be loyal to the Lord.

If his nation was to prosper in peace, Joshua realized it could be accomplished only by careful compliance with God's will— not by subtle or cunning human diplomacy. It is a tremendous tribute to Joshua that he constantly centered the attention of his contemporaries on the character of God rather than on his own personal charisma.

To this end, and for this precise purpose, Joshua in his old age and declining strength summoned all the local leaders, chieftains and military officers to his home. Once again he intended to remind them earnestly of their obligations to God. He knew full well that Israel was a stiff-necked, difficult race to govern. He knew from firsthand experience in the wilderness how readily they could go astray. He had been a personal witness to the terrible tragedies that overtook this intransigent people when they grumbled and rebelled against their God.

Lest this should ever happen again in his lifetime, Joshua now addressed the leaders of Israel with enormous earnestness. He warned them in ominous terms of the risks they ran in ever rejecting God. He pointed out the appalling perils they faced if ever they deviated from the laws of the Lord. He reminded them once more of the utter ruin that would befall their nation and people if they defied the will of God. He told of the inevitable disasters that would come upon them if they became embroiled with the evil practices of the pagan people they had overrun and supplanted.

The declarations thundering out from this loyal, old war-
horse may seem to some stern, severe and terribly tough. His
was essentially the cry of a prophet calling his people to a full
commitment to the Most High. Like clear, pure, piercing bugle notes they were unmistakable in their meaning; awesome
in their warning:
1) *Do not turn away from God's word!*
2) *Do not accommodate yourself to the world's ways!*
3) *Do not give your allegiance to false gods!*
4) *Do not set your will to serve other idols!*
5) *Do not become subject to their deception!*
6) *Do not adopt the life style of the pagan people!*
7) *Do not marry or form misalliances among them!*
To do so would be to become as a prey taken in a trap. It
would be as a bird caught in a snare. The end would be pain,
ruin, blindness and total deception ending in destruction.

Happily for both Joshua and for Israel, his pronouncements
were taken very seriously. His people did not deviate in their
devotion to the Lord. So to the end of his rich, long life they
reveled in peace and prosperity just as he had predicted.

The same identical spiritual principles delineated so clearly
by Joshua for the conduct of his people have never altered or
diminished in their authenticity. They apply as much to modern man in the twentieth century as they did to Israel in 1427
B.C. Three thousand four hundred years of human history have
not eroded their validity one iota.

Anyone who is at all familiar with Israel's subsequent record
is dismayed by the utter degradation and unmitigated disasters
which overtook this nation when it forsook God. It makes for
some of the most dismal reading in human history. The chroni-
cle of Israel's judges, her wretched kings, her pleading prophets is shot through with remorse, shame and ignominy.

But the same may be said for a nation like Great Britain. At
the turn of this century Britain gloried in her name as "The

People of the Book." The British Isles were a bastion of Christianity, a land where God's Word was revered, read, honored and obeyed. Under the rule of devout and godly monarchs the might and influence of Britain encircled the globe. The sun never set on the Union Jack.

Under her protection, power and justice, missionary enterprise flourished across the whole earth. Uncounted millions came to hear the great Good News of God's love in Christ.

But by degrees Britain forsook the God of her forefathers. She turned more and more to her own wretched ways. Today she stands stripped and shorn of her former greatness, a weak and hapless people who once knew great glory.

Precisely the same dreadful decline may very well overtake the United States of America if she repudiates her God and rejects His righteous precepts.

And, I must add, the identical end awaits any individual who chooses to do likewise.

20

Joshua's Last Challenge to His People

JOSHUA HAD COME to the sunset of his day. The long and illustrious record of his exploits for God and for his generation were culminating in a blaze of splendor, equal to the stirring spectacle of a golden sunset gilding the western sky. In one final burst of magnificent honor to God he summoned all of Israel to Shechem.

Here he was now, a gnarled and noble veteran of 110 years. He had spent 40 of those years as a sweating slave, abused and brutalized by the Egyptians, in the slime pits along the Nile. Then he had spent the next 40 years as Moses' lieutenant in the dreadful wilderness wanderings where all but his friend, Caleb, and himself died in the desert wastes. Finally his last 30 years had been spent in this glorious land of promised abundance. Here the Almighty Lord of Hosts had granted him great victory over the Canaanites and at last peace, prosperity and rest from his foes.

These last seventy years were surely the most stupendous, the most remarkable, yet at the same time the most terrible in all of Israel's tangled history. All through the centuries yet to come, this wayward race would look back upon this period of time as the most formidable in God's dealing with them. Their poets, their prophets and their historians would always and ever remind the Hebrews of the horrendous events that brought Israel from abject bondage to a place of glorious power as a magnificent empire in the Middle East.

Just as Moses, the first mighty prophet in Israel, had rehearsed to his compatriots what God had done for them, when he came to the end of his life, so likewise now did Joshua. These leaders saw clearly, with undimmed vision, that it was the Most High who had delivered Israel. And this vivid, stirring, spiritual perspective was now to be pressed upon the people again.

Deliberately, and with a fine sense of drama, Joshua summoned all of Israel to Shechem again. Shechem means, "The place of diligence, of perseverance, of faithfulness, of loyal fidelity." Here in this beautiful, grassy amphitheater lying warm to the sun Joshua would challenge Israel for a last time to present themselves to the Most High.

Thirty years before, Joshua had assembled all of his people in this very place. After their remarkable crossing of Jordan, their victory over Jericho and the conquest of Ai he had summoned them to this spot. Here he erected his altar of rough field rocks on which to offer sacrifices of praise and gratitude to God. Here he read in the hearing of all Israel the laws of the Lord.

Shechem was the place which was first laid claim to by Abraham when he came to Canaan from beyond the far-off river delta of the Euphrates. Shechem was where God had given His promise of possessing all this land. Shechem was where Jacob erected his sacred altar and called it "ELELOHE–ISRAEL"— God, the Lord Jehovah of Israel is here (Genesis 33:18–20).

Lifting his voice now in thundering tones Joshua speaks on behalf of the Most High. He rehearses in sharp, stabbing sentences all the exploits of the Eternal One. Beginning with

God's call to Abraham in Ur of the Chaldees, he recounts in stirring notes all the wondrous ways in which the Lord led His people down to this very day.

Seventeen times in rapid-fire succession Joshua shouts aloud for the Lord with bugle-like blasts: *"I took your father Abraham from across the flood—I gave unto Isaac the sons of Jacob and Esau—I sent Moses and Aaron to Egypt—I plagued the Egyptians—I brought your fathers out of bondage—I led you into the Land of Promise—I drove out the Amorites before you—I have given you this land. . . ."*

Anointed with the very presence and power of God's own Spirit, Joshua does not flinch from speaking for Jehovah with zealous fervor and burning courage. Vehemently he asserts that all the conquests, all the miracles, all the remarkable advances made by Israel were essentially the work of God and not of men.

Even at the risk of alienating all his associates, Joshua presses this point home with enormous emphasis. *"It is not with your sword or with your bows that the enemy has been vanquished—but by the power of God!"*

His eyes blazing like lamps lit with celestial fire, the aged veteran lifts up his sun-browned arms and stretches them out across the countryside. His voice thundering like a mighty summer storm he shouts to all of Israel: *"I (God, very God) have given you a land for which you did not labor . . . cities to dwell in which you did not build . . . vineyards and olive groves to relish which you did not plant."*

All of this was God's doing and not man's!

It was a sobering, solemn, humbling moment.

A great stillness swept across the crowd.

A mystical hush fell upon the people.

They saw themselves stripped of all their pride before God.

Joshua speaking with the unction of the Most High upon him stood stark and grand before them.

They had never seen him garbed in greater glory.

He was at the end of his days but at the pinnacle of power under the hand of God.

Again his voice thundered and reverberated throughout the amphitheater: *"Now, therefore, fear the Lord . . . serve Him in sincerity and in truth . . . put away every false and foreign God from among you . . . and choose. Decide, determine once and for all to whom you will be loyal!"*

There was another awesome pause. A profound moment of truth confronted the congregation. They had been challenged to make an irrevocable choice. Israel, as of old, was being called to total commitment.

Would it be to choose the Lord God, Jehovah, or would it be to settle for servitude to the pagan deities of deception around them?

They were a chosen people. Israel was God's special treasure.

Would they now choose God? Would He become their treasure?

In another thunderclap of frightening force and awesome majesty Joshua sounded a last stirring note, *"As for me and for my house, we will serve the Lord"* (Joshua 24:15).

It was a climactic call to utter dedication.

It was a clear trumpet note of unmistakable sound.

It was a closing challenge to Israel and to all of us.

"Decide this day what you will do with God!"

Joshua was unashamed of where he stood.

His whole life had been a demonstration of single-minded devotion to God. His loyalty had been of the highest order. His bold obedience had set a supreme standard for all to emulate. His faithfulness to the Lord in the face of formidable odds had never wavered. His entire career had burned as a flame of fearless faith for others to follow.

Yet amid all of this Joshua never took the honor to himself.

He was never, ever, prone to pride because of his exalted position as the commander of God's chosen people. He was never corrupted by the power bestowed upon him. He was never a general to gloat over the victories granted to him by God.

Always, ever, Joshua had humility of heart and wisdom of mind to see that all of his magnificent achievements were in reality the work of God. He was sensitive enough in spirit to see clearly that all he had accomplished was because of the power and presence of the Most High active in his affairs.

Because of this contrite character God had honored Joshua with incredible conquests. Because of his simple, forthright faith in God, mountains of obstruction had been removed in the invasion of Canaan. Because of his undeviating devotion to God and ready compliance with His commands, Israel's hapless desert days had been turned into thrilling triumphs. God had given them sweeping territory with a rich abundance of benefits because He alone could bring blessing out of bareness.

What was true for Joshua and for Israel three thousand years ago can be equally true for the Church today. The same spiritual principles which operated then are still in force today. The cardinal concepts that made Joshua an overcomer can move us Christian to conquests in the twentieth century.

Because these are not often clearly taught in our churches, I wish to pause here briefly and put them into layman's language for the benefit of the reader. As God's people we are not challenged enough to great exploits under God as Joshua did for Israel. Too often the approach of modern preachers in the pulpit is one of a "holding pattern." Too often people are given the impression that to be a Christian is to be always under attack. Too often we are inundated with instructions on how to barely "hold our own" against the onslaught of the enemy.

Christ does not call us to this "fortresslike" life style.

He does not commit us to a cloistered cell.

He does not commission us to a fixed position.
God challenges us to lives of fearless faith in Himself.
He calls us to take territory in great triumphs.
He commissions us to go out into all the world in victory.
Where the obstruction lies in all of this is our woeful lack of understanding of the basic principles enunciated to Israel by Joshua on this memorable occasion at Shechem. For purposes of clarity, simplicity and comprehension they are here put in a form that anyone with spiritual understanding can lay hold of and live by in victory.

1) It is God Himself who in His sovereignty chooses a person or people for His own purposes. He did this with Abraham; He did it with Israel; He did it with Joshua. He wants to do it with you if you will allow Him.

"Praise be to the God and Father of our Lord Jesus Christ for giving us through Christ every possible spiritual benefit as citizens of Heaven! For consider what he has done— before the foundation of the world he chose us to become, in Christ, his holy and blameless children living within his constant care.

He planned, in his purpose of love, that we should be adopted as his own children through Jesus Christ—that we might learn to praise that glorious generosity of his which has made us welcome in the everlasting love he bears towards the Beloved" (Ephesians 1:3–5, Phillips).

2) Our Father chooses to do this, not because we deserve it, or have merited such a privilege, but because He loves us. He has our best interests in mind. Also, He has His own wondrous purposes to carry out in our affairs.

3) Having so selected us and drawn us to Himself, He knows full well all our failings and tendency to go wrong. He calls to us even though we are sinners. He chooses us even though we are

far from Him. He entreats us to respond in trust to His overtures. He invites us to accept His pardon, His forgiveness, His
acceptance . . . *not because we are by nature great people, but
because He is a great God.*

4) As we come into His family, become His children, sense
His Spirit at work within our spirits re-creating us, we are
humbled and broken by His lovingkindness and abundant generosity. We become increasingly aware that it is not *who we
are* that counts, but rather *Whose we are!* Israel was never a
great or unique people simply by birth or tradition, but rather
because they were God's treasure, chosen, called and owned
by Jehovah.

5) There begins to break in upon the person who responds to
God's call a growing awareness of his own undone condition.
Despite our past wrongs, despite our sinister sinfulness, de-
spite our waywardness, Christ can cleanse us from our faults.
He not only forgives but He forgets our failings. He bestows all
His benefits on us in abundance. He plucks us from the slime
pits and sets us free to stand on our feet and follow Him.

6) His compelling compassion and overriding condescension
compel Him to come alongside us to deliver us from our dilemma. He wants to see us liberated. He wants us freed from
slavery to the enemy of our souls, from sin, yes, and eventually
even from bondage to our strong-willed selves. He did this for
Israel in Egypt. He wants to do it for us!

7) To achieve this He performs mighty miracles in our lives.
He makes the impossible possible. He will lead us unerringly if
we will allow Him. He will shelter and protect us if we will
comply with His wishes. He will supply wisdom and discernment for the way which we never experienced before. These
are all of His arrangement, just as were the cloud by day, the
fire by night, the manna at dawn for Israel.

8) Amid all of these activities it is utterly imperative for us to
grasp that it is God who is at work behind the scenes. It is

Christ Himself who does for us exceedingly far beyond anything we might have expected. This realization then should pulverize any pride we have in our own talents, abilities or strategies. Slowly but surely we come to see that it is not our skills that ensure success, but His. So in humility and gratitude we gladly comply with His wishes and cooperate with His commands.

9) To live thus is to live in quiet faith in Christ. It is to come to the conclusion that under His control we can be conquerors. It is He who by His Spirit working in us empowers us to move out boldly to take territory for Him. It is He who prepares a way for us through impossible places. It is He who enables us to possess our possessions which He has provided on our behalf.

10) So it is, that because of our Father's great faithfulness to us we come into lives that are fruitful, productive and abundant. Over and beyond even this He brings us into the sweet benefit of rest and quiet repose—the place of peace. The past is all behind us; only the glory and grandeur of His goodness lies ahead for us. *Bless His wondrous name!*

11) In all of this we do not gloat over the victories granted to us by our Lord. We do not become arrogant in attitude; spiritually proud. Rather, the reverse. Increasingly we realize that every good, every achievement, every conquest comes to us as a gift from God, not a triumph of our own strength!

12) Awed at the wondrous work of God, we give ourselves to Him gladly, eagerly, energetically. We abandon ourselves totally to His purposes. We divest ourselves completely from any sort of allegiance to the sordid society in which we live. We are done forever with the "false gods" of duplicity and deception that surround us on all sides.

13) We go on by deliberate, daily choices to follow Christ in fearless faith just as Joshua did. It may not make us popular, but it surely will make us the powerful people of God, who, with banners flying, will storm the strongholds of sin and evil.

We will become that courageous church under whose fierce assault the gates of hell will crumble in confusion.

14) Forgetting those things which are behind us—our fears, our failures, our lack of faithfulness—we push on triumphantly until the call comes ringing in our ears, "Come home, come home! Well done, good and faithful servant!" As we have chosen to serve Christ on earth, He chooses then to bestow on us all the benefits of heaven.

21

A Fitting Farewell

IT IS MOVING for us to observe how so many of God's great saints had an acute awareness of the day of their own departure from earth. Walking with the Almighty in intimate communion and joyous harmony they knew assuredly of their call home.

Joshua was now ready for his leave-taking.

During his illustrious leadership all of Israel had obeyed God.

The last years of his life were replete with rest, honor and the well-earned respect of a national hero.

But, before his departure, he endeavored, under God, to extract a solemn commitment from Israel that after his death they would continue to serve the Lord. Perhaps it was remotely possible that out of a sense of loyalty to himself, as well as to God, this obdurate nation might just continue to honor the Most High who had been so faithful to them. At least it was a hope he held in his heart.

Surprisingly enough, standing before the massed multitude in the lovely vale of Shechem he heard the shout rise three times from a hundred thousand throats: *"We will serve the Lord, He is our God!"* Thrice the sounds went winging on the wind. Three times over, the triumphant shout rose above the crowd like the trumpet blasts of a glorious victory. *"We will serve the Lord Jehovah, He is our God!"* . . . . then again: *"We will serve the Lord, He is our God!"*

Joshua was never an idle dreamer.

He was not a man easily swayed by public sentiment.

He was not a novice in understanding human nature.

All too vividly, painfully, sadly he recalled those same syllables shouted in unison by Israel at the base of Mount Sinai. There, too, at the foot of that formidable mountain, Israel had declared loyal allegiance to God.

Yet, within six weeks they were clamoring for Aaron to fashion them a bull calf from the gold off their own bodies. In less than a year, after being too terrified to enter the land of promise, they would demand to be led back to Egypt under a new leader. And for another forty years this intransigent people would wander hopelessly in the wilderness of their divided loyalties.

No, no, no! Joshua knew full well that in their folly and futility Israel would not long serve God after he was gone. He realized that there was ever present within the social life of his people the tendency to be subverted by the pagan practices of the Canaanites. He was astute enough to know that spiritually they would never stand against the subtle subversion of the false gods around them.

Bluntly and boldly he addressed them with the last of his strength: *"You cannot serve the Lord"* (Joshua 24:19).

No doubt it shattered their self-assurance.

It may have seemed too harsh a statement.

Perhaps it was intended to make them aware of the great peril in which they stood when he passed from them.

Despite their insistence that they would not forsake the Lord, Joshua for a last time reminded them briefly but solemnly of their options.

"Obey God in humility and fidelity and you will flourish! Forsake Him and you will perish!"

This was true privately as individuals, and collectively as an entire nation.

Tragic as it may seem to us now in retrospect, the subsequent history of Israel was to be one of dire disaster. First under a succession of judges, then later under a motley array of unstable kings, this people was to sink into dreadful degradation. Ultimately they would end up in bondage again, scattered to the four winds of the world.

As if to bind the nation to their promises, Joshua then proceeded to erect a huge rock as a lasting memorial to this monumental day in Israel's history. This was an ancient custom. It had been done by Jacob at Bethel. It was a rite carried out at Mizpah. It was to be done in later years at Ebenezer.

The inherent idea in the establishment of a stone memorial as a witness to a compact was fairly simple, even for the most ordinary people to grasp. The enduring, permanent quality of the stone stood as a witness that would outlast all of their years. It was a durable symbol that would stand throughout all generations bearing witness to the solemn commitment made on this sacred occasion.

Israel's posterity could always come back to this spot to be reminded of the binding vows made by their fathers that they would be faithful to God. It was Joshua's ardent hope that the erection of such a memorial, under the old gnarled oak, would somehow assure Israel of some stability in its stormy story.

With somber face and in deliberate decisiveness Joshua wrote out the serious statements of his people and placed them in safekeeping by the rock. They were to remain there as an indelible witness to this day on which all of Israel again declared its undivided loyalty and allegiance to the Lord.

Joshua could do no more as a man.

He had brought all of his people out of the wilderness into the Promised Land. Under God's great hand he had led them in triumph to take all the territory given to them by the Most High. There they had found not only peace, but also abundant prosperity. Joshua had brought all of Israel to a point of total commitment to God.

It was a remarkable record of achievement.

Now he was bidding them all a fond farewell.

Each family was free to return in quietness to their own home. It would be up to them whether or not they would indeed honor their vows to God.

Joshua died at the remarkable age of 110 years.

He was buried with great dignity on the mountain he himself had claimed as his inheritance.

There in Timnath-Serah this gallant general, of formidable faith in God, found his final rest in the place of abundance and fruitfulness.

It marked the end of an epic era for Israel as a nation. Because of one man's fearless faith in the Almighty, this entire people had been brought from abject poverty to a pinnacle of power and prosperity under God.

Not only had Joshua achieved amazing exploits for himself as a man, but also he had brought all of his people to remarkable rest in the care of the Almighty.

No leader ever started out with so little and concluded with so much. Joshua had taken a shattered, woebegone, weary band of stragglers in the desert wastes and forged them into a formidable Middle Eastern empire.

He has seldom been given the full credit he deserves as perhaps the greatest man of faith ever to set foot on the stage of human history. In fact, his entire brilliant career was a straightforward story of simply setting down one foot after another in quiet compliance with the commands of his God. So he moved ahead steadily from one step of triumph to the next.

Perhaps it is because Joshua was never a man given to flamboyancy or theatrics that his name is often by-passed amid the more glamorous and grandiose of Israel's leaders. This is often the way with the world.

The quiet, solid, reliable individuals are overlooked. Yet ultimately it is they who are the sterling characters who achieve great exploits with God in their generation.

Reflecting quietly upon the life of Joshua, there sweeps into my own spirit an enormous longing to become a man somewhat of his caliber. And it is my ardent hope that the same may be true to some degree of you the reader.

We live in a day, when as of old, God is looking for men and women of fearless faith, who will step out to achieve great things for Him. God has not changed since the time of Joshua, nor does He honor faith less now than He did then. It is simply a case of coming to a place where we will walk with Christ by faith rather than by sight.

As we open our lives to the unrestricted incoming of His presence, it is possible for us to know all the wondrous fullness of God's gracious Spirit. As we permit Him to exercise His wondrous control of our careers we, too, can fully expect to see remarkable results in our day-to-day experiences. Yet over and beyond all of this, there will go on the beautiful transformation of our characters into the likeness of our Lord.

These are not just idle daydreams.

They are not just wishful thinking.

They are not just elusive hopes.

For all of us as Christians they can be the warp and woof of the fabric woven from our lives with God. He it is who can take us common people and turn us into triumphant overcomers as we trust Him.

He it is who can cause us to be victorious warriors in the world. He it is who can bring us into an abundant life of fruitfulness both for ourselves and others. He it is who can enable us to find our fulfillment, rest and contentment in Christ.

On our part it calls for compliance with His Word, constant communion with His Spirit, an unshakable confidence in His great care for us throughout all of time and eternity.

IN *GOD IS MY DELIGHT* THE AUTHOR BARES HIS
OWN HEART AS HE SHARES WHAT HE HAS LEARNED
IN A LIFETIME OF WALKING WITH GOD.

WHAT REVIEWERS SAY ABOUT *GOD IS MY DELIGHT*

" . . . a rich feast. I like portraits of those who enjoy the Lord. They do more to commend the gospel to people than anything else I can think of. Blessed are those lives that leave us watching wistfully, and longing to know the Lord better!"

William C. Brownson
Broadcast Minister, Words of Hope

"Phillip Keller's spiritual autobiography is like fresh air! Here is a man—a real man with warts and all—who loves God and has an intimate relationship with Him. It is not only interesting in content— it is inspiring. After reading it, I am motivated to know, love and serve God better."

Steve Brown
KeyLife Network

"In reading *God Is My Delight*, I discovered a person who has walked with God and has himself caught this discovery from others who have walked with God. Isn't that the very core of Christian living and witnessing? Too often we restrict witnessing to the words we speak on behalf of God. But I think an even more powerful witnessing is the way we role model a God of delight in our lives—a presence so obvious and winsome that others will hunger and thirst for Him."

V. Gilbert Beers, President
Scripture Press Publications
Former Editor of *Christianity Today* Magazine

"Keller seeks to nurture our souls in Godliness by opening his own heart to us. Reflecting autobiographically, he makes himself vulnerable to our scrutiny and shares his own life pilgrimage of expanding faith, joy, and peace. As we see the growing delight he finds in fellowship with the triune God, our hunger and thirst for righteousness grows. Keller succeeds in sharing his delight with us as he guides us to a richer, sweeter fellowship with the loving Father, Christ, and Holy Spirit."

George K. Brushaber, President
Bethel College and Seminary

"Those who have profited as I have from Phillip Keller's earlier works . . . will want to reflect carefully upon the author's affirmations in this new book, *God Is My Delight*. Even those most knowledgeable in biblical truth often feel inadequacy in their daily walk with God. The thought-provoking concepts in *God Is My Delight* will challenge every reader to experience more of who God is and what He provides."

Dr. Homer A. Kent, Professor Emeritus and Former President
Grace Theological Seminary

"Poor people need to take rich people out to dinner and listen because success leaves clues. Those who hunger and thirst after God, those who feel poverty-stricken before God would delight to sit and listen, to absorb the riches of Keller's faith, his intimacy with his God. *God Is My Delight* lets you do that! It's one of those books you can't put down. He strikes a chord deep within us."

Dr. Joseph C. Aldridge, President
Multnomah School of the Bible

" . . . Keller distills the wisdom of his seventy years to portray a positive relationship to God as loving Father, dearest Friend (Christ), and Counselor (Holy Spirit). His trinitarian approach is not only orthodox, but a pleasant antidote to contemporary views of God that either deny His existence entirely, or erect formidable barriers to any closeness with the Creator that could regard Him as a 'Friend' in any sense. In this spiritual autobiography, Keller rather enjoys God in the awesome spheres of nature, in the saving nature of His Word, and in the encouragement of the Spirit."

Dr. Paul L. Maier, Professor of History
Western Michigan University

" . . . a precious, heart-warming delight to my own soul. What a glorious tribute to the triune God this volume is."

Dr. W.A. Criswell, Pastor
First Baptist Church, Dallas, TX

"There can be no better knowledge than that of knowing God as the Loving Father and Jesus Christ as the dearest Friend and to be guided and counseled by the Holy Spirit. A book of this nature surely expresses the heart of a true shepherd, restoring the souls of the sheep as they bask in the love of the heavenly Father."

Pastor Chuck Smith
Calvary Chapel, Costa Mesa, CA

"When a man with such a rich life has walked with the Lord as long as Phillip Keller has, you anticipate he will have something to say. *God Is My Delight* is sprinkled with human interest in such a way that the reader will share in Keller's life and thus share in his delight for God."

Dr. Woodrow Kroll, General Director
Back to the Bible

"As they have for years, Phillip Keller's writings continue to 'shepherd' people—that is, they *lead* you to the waters of refreshing and feed you in the pastures of enrichment. *God Is My Delight* is, *delightfully*, more of the same."

Jack W. Hayford, D.Litt., Senior Pastor
The Church On the Way, Van Nuys, CA

"Mr. Keller has a great gift of making profound things understandable and bringing things of heaven down to where people live on earth. He has done it again in *God Is My Delight*."

D. Stuart Briscoe, Pastor
Elmbrook Church, Waukesha, WI

"With this book, *God Is My Delight*, Phillip Keller has described the simple essence of our life and joy: an intimate relationship with God. Keller acquaints us with three people in his life who embodied the Lord's love, and so taught him many lessons about the meaning of everyday life lived in vital relationship with the Lord. I found his book a welcome and refreshing respite from modern life's pressures and preoccupations, reminding me again that the best part of life is to rest, like Mary, at the feet of our loving Lord and Master."

Mark O. Hatfield
United States Senator

CPSIA information can be obtained
at www.ICGtesting.com
Printed in the USA
FSOW03n0740291015
12747FS